The Parish in Catholic Tradition

History, Theology and Canon Law

D0877853

James A. Coriden

1.) Intro 1-3
2)   ch 4
2.)   5-9

PAULIST PRESS
New York • Mahwah, N.J.

Cover design by John Gummere.

Library of Congress Cataloging-in-Publication Data

Coriden, James A.
  The parish in Catholic tradition : history, theology, and canon law / James A. Coriden
    p.   cm.
  Includes bibliographical references and index.
  ISBN 0-8091-3685-6 (alk. paper)
  1. Parishes. 2. Catholic Church—Government. 3. Parishes (Canon law).
  4. Parishes—United States. 5. Pastoral theology—Catholic Church. I. Title.
  BX1934.C67 1996
  250'.8'822—dc20   96-33120
                                                                              CIP

Published by Paulist Press
997 Macarthur Boulevard
Mahwah, New Jersey 07430

Printed and bound in the
United States of America

Contents

Abbreviations

AA   *Apostolicam Actuositatem,* Decree on the Apostolate of the Laity, Second Vatican Council, November 18, 1965.

AG   *Ad Gentes,* Decree on the Church's Missionary Activity, Second Vatican Council, December 7, 1965.

c., cc. Canon, canons, Code of Canon Law, Pope John Paul II, January 25, 1983.

CA   *Centesimus Annus,* Encyclical Letter on the One Hundredth Anniversary of *Rerum Novarum,* Pope John Paul II, May 1, 1991.

CD   *Christus Dominus,* Decree on the Bishops' Pastoral Office in the Church, Second Vatican Council, October 28, 1965.

CL   *Christifideles Laici,* Apostolic Exhortation on the Laity, Pope John Paul II, December 30, 1988.

DH   *Dignitatis Humanae,* Declaration on Religious Freedom, Second Vatican Council, December 7, 1965.

FC   *Familiaris Consortio,* Apostolic Exhortation on the Family, Pope John Paul II, December 15, 1981.

LG   *Lumen Gentium,* Dogmatic Constitution on the Church, Second Vatican Council, November 21, 1964.

MM   *Mater et Magistra,* Encyclical Letter on a Reevaluation of the Social Question, Pope John XXIII, May 15, 1961.

QA   *Quadragesimo Anno,* Encyclical Letter on the Fortieth Anniversary of *Rerum Novarum,* Pope Pius XI, May 15, 1931.

RN   *Rerum Novarum,* Encyclical Letter on the Conditions of Workers, Pope Leo XIII, May 15, 1891.

SC   *Sacrosanctum Concilium,* Constitution on the Sacred Liturgy, Second Vatican Council, December 4, 1963.

SRS   *Sollicitudo Rei Socialis,* Encyclical Letter on the Twentieth Anniversary of *Populorum Progressio,* Pope John Paul II, December 30, 1987.

Introduction

The Purpose and Scope of the Book

This is a book about local Roman Catholic churches. These local congregations are most frequently called parishes. Other forms of local church communities, such as mission churches and campus communities, are also common in the Catholic tradition, and they are included here.

This volume intends to present a background and a context for contemporary Catholic parishes. The background is biblical, historical, theological and canonical. The context is ministerial, relational and legal. The book allows the reader to reach an accurate understanding of the authentic nature and function of parishes within the Catholic tradition.

Much of what is said about Catholic parishes here applies as well to the local congregations in other Christian traditions. The sections on biblical origins, much of the history and theology of local churches, the relational and American legal portions of the study will be of interest to readers from Protestant and Orthodox churches.

The book is aimed at all those who have an interest in their local church. It should assist those who minister in Catholic parishes, as well as those preparing to do so, priests, sisters, laypersons, deacons, seminarians and religious brothers. It is directed at those laypersons who are actively involved in the life of their parishes or who are thinking of getting involved. Members of parish pastoral councils, especially when newly elected and beginning their term of service, will benefit from

1

reading this book. It will inform them about their tradition and orient them to their task.

What it is Not about

It is important to be clear about what the book is not. It is not a how-to book about doing parish ministry. It is not a survey about the current status of parishes or what does or does not work in pastoral care. Nor is the book a commentary on the canon law of parishes, though it contains much from the canonical tradition.

This is a book about parishes—their origins, historical development, theological nature and canonical organization. It includes an emphasis on the canonical rights and obligations of local Catholic communities, and it summarizes the American law that applies to them. It treats of the necessary activities of parish communities and the structures of pastoral ministry within them.

The book is about the identity, dignity and stability of Catholic parishes. It draws upon many scholarly works and tries to make them accessible to interested parishioners and ministers. It contains no footnotes, but ample sources and additional readings are supplied.

An Overview

The volume begins with a look at the local communities of Christians as they are pictured in the New Testament. As those earliest churches formed and spread, they borrowed from their surrounding cultures and gradually developed patterns of communion and ministry that endured.

Next comes a survey of the history of parishes. The first churches were in the cities and towns of the Roman Empire, but soon they spread into villages and rural areas. The congregations took on different organizational forms under the pressure of various historical forces, for example, the early baptismal churches, later proprietary churches and medieval collegiate churches.

Reform movements in the church greatly influenced parish life, and so did the vast missionary efforts of the sixteenth century. The rise of modern states, the industrial revolution and the growth of large cities impacted on parishes and ministry within them. America experienced the planting and growth of Catholic parishes in its own unique way.

The theology of the local church arrived late, but in the twentieth century it evolved, rapidly matured and became strong. The Second Vatican Council solidified and advanced this development, and its clarification has continued since the council.

Local church imp

The social teachings of the church in the modern era have supported and strengthened the rightful place of the parish, especially the teachings on the right of association, the common good and the principles of solidarity and subsidiarity.

The book takes a canonical turn in the <u>fifth and following</u> chapters. First it explores the nature and activities of parishes as they are expressed in the canons, the church's rules of governance. Then the rights and obligations of parish communities are newly enumerated and explained. Finally, the study addresses the defense or vindication of those parish rights and duties, who can do it and how.

ch 5,6,7 canonical

<u>Pastoral ministry</u> within the local church is sketched in the eighth chapter. It outlines canonical elements of pastoral care and presents some new possibilities for organizing parish ministries.

ch 8 pastoral ministry.

Parishes have various relationships to other communities, for example, the diocesan church, neighboring Catholic parishes, nearby Protestant churches and the surrounding civic and political communities. These are touched on in <u>Chapter</u> 9.

Relations ch 9

The book closes with an overview of the parish in American civil law. Various areas of federal, state and local laws impact on the life of local Catholic communities, and a first level of awareness of that impact may help in parish planning and ministry.

Some case studies are appended to the book as learning and discussion exercises. A parish council could engage some of them in the process of its own formation. It may be liberating to reflect on someone else's problems rather than those close to home!

Parishes and Dioceses

Diocese

In the Roman Catholic scheme of things the church headed by the bishop is called a "diocese" (a name borrowed from an administrative unit within the Roman Empire). Canonically dioceses are called "particular churches," as opposed to the universal church headed by the pope and the college of bishops. A diocese is really a communion of local parish churches, just as the universal church is a communion of particular churches.

Over the last several decades in the United States more and more functions of parish churches have been assumed by the diocesan church. A process of centralization has been set in motion that has changed the relationship of parishes and dioceses. A few examples will illustrate this trend:

1. Earlier communities of Catholics would form and then purchase property for their church and other buildings. Now dioceses often purchase land in connection with real estate developments even before any residential community is in place.

2. Parishes used to borrow money for construction of their buildings from the local bank. Now more frequently the parish borrows money from the diocese, which serves as a central bank, using the deposits of money from other parishes.

3. Pastors commonly obtained fire and accident insurance from a local insurance agent, often a parishioner. Now many dioceses are self-insured and provide insurance for all of the parishes in the diocese.

4. Purchases of services and supplies for local parishes in earlier times were made locally, from neighborhood merchants. Now some larger dioceses have central purchasing agencies that make goods, from automobiles to toilet paper, available to parishes.

5. Formerly parish schools, catechetical programs and many other services were relatively autonomous and self-reliant. Now they are heavily regulated, controlled and assisted by the diocese.

6. In the past the long-term tenure of pastors lent a stability and familiarity to parishes. Now the terms of pastors are strictly limited, and pastoral changes are relatively frequent.

7. Parishes used to endure for many decades; they were relatively permanent and lived on after their membership had drastically changed or declined. The new powers given to the diocesan bishops permit parishes to be suppressed or merged easily, and in some dioceses this has happened to scores of parishes.

These illustrations reveal a mixed blessing. They make sense in terms of highly prized American efficiency, and they often result in some fiscal economies. That's the positive side of the blessing. The negative side is a diminished sense of local church. The legitimate autonomy of local congregations can be compromised by this centralizing trend. This will occur almost certainly unless the local churches' legitimate autonomy and self-direction are understood, appreciated and asserted.

To put it another way, this centralizing tendency within the diocesan churches causes bishops and chancery officials to think and act like corporate managers and to treat parishes like branch offices or local franchises of that corporation. A subtle denigration of the rightful dignity, stability and cohesion of the local churches can result. Parishes are not local outlets of a corporate chain. They are local churches, fully and authentically, just as the local churches named in the New Testament were.

One further point to consider is that centralization is the opposite of subsidiarity. The principle of subsidiary function, which is one of the foundation stones of Catholic social teaching, requires that the local churches be respected as such and allowed a maximum range of self-determination. *Principle of Subsidiary Function.*

Parishes as Communities

Parishes have always presupposed a human community gathered together in faith. At times primary attention was given to the territory of the parish, or to the church building, or to the pastor's role and rights in the parish or to the endowment that supported him. Currently the notion of community is clearly in the forefront of the church's vision of what a parish is. A parish is now officially described in the Code of Canon Law as "a defined *community* of the Christian faithful established on a stable basis within a particular church" (c. 515.1). This book speaks often about the parish as community. It might be helpful at the outset to clarify the meaning of *community*. The term *community* is used here in a wider and more general sense than in the sociological sense of a close-knit and integrated social system in which everyone knows everyone else and their interactions are frequent, manifold and personal, as, for example, in a monastery or small village. *Parish Defined!!*

Community is said to (1) develop a sense of belonging and loyalty, (2) empower action in common and (3) nurture values and standards for its members as part of their moral consensus. Everyone recognizes that these things are achieved in different degrees, that community is realized at various levels.

Some rural, small-town or urban ethnic parishes may indeed fit these sociological descriptions of primary communities. But many urban and suburban Catholic parishes are much larger, more diverse, more heterogeneous and less intimate than this. These parishes may contain several communities or subdivisions or subgroups within their boundaries. Some neighborhoods, language or nationality groups, the parents of the school children or those who always attend the nine o'clock mass may achieve something closer to a primary community.

Catholic parishes themselves are more often secondary groupings—social aggregates or associational types of structures—than truly integrated primary communities.

Just as there are different levels of community, there are different levels of participation in parish communities. Joseph Fichter, the well-known Jesuit sociologist, divided parishioners into four types:

1. "nuclear," the most active and loyal parish members (perhaps 5 to 10 percent of the total);

2. "modal," the large majority of ordinary practicing Catholics (more like 70 to 80 percent);

3. "marginal," those whose observance is minimal;

4. "lapsed," Catholics who do not practice their religion but have not joined another. There is no illusion that all Catholics are equally faithful and enthusiastic members of their congregations.

Parish community, then, in this book is used in the broader, canonical sense that refers to local churches whose members have varying degrees of participation and mutual interaction, of commitment and active engagement.

Acknowledgments

The author is indebted to many other authors for various facts and ideas in this book. Since the work is intended for a general audience rather than a scholarly one, the English language sources are indicated at the end of each chapter along with suggested further readings.

Many foreign-language studies were used as well, but, because of their inaccesibility, they are not noted. One does deserve special mention: the fine book *De Paroecia,* by the Italian canonist Francesco Coccopalmerio (Rome: Editrice Pontificia Universita Gregoriana, 1991).

Small portions of chapters 1 through 4 and major portions of chapters 6 and 7 were derived from the author's previously published articles: "The Foundations of the Rights of Parishes: The Bases for the Canonical Rights of Parishes and Other Local Catholic Communities" in *Ius in Vita et in Missione Ecclesiae* (Vatican City: Editrice Libreria Vaticana, 1994), pp. 505–25; "The Rights of Parishes," *Studia Canonica* 28 (1994): pp. 293–309; "The Vindication of Parish Rights," *The Jurist* 54, 1 (1994): pp. 22–39.

Sources and Readings

On the sociology of the parish:

Blochlinger, A. *The Modern Parish Community.* New York: P.J. Kenedy & Sons, 1965, pp. 172–216.

Carrier, H. *The Sociology of Religious Belonging.* London: Dartman, Longman & Todd, 1965.

Castelli, J., and J. Gremillion. *The Emerging Parish: The Notre Dame Study of Catholic Life Since Vatican II.* San Francisco: Harper & Row, 1987.

Fichter, J. *Social Relations in the Urban Parish.* Chicago: University of Chicago Press, 1954.

————. *Southern Parish.* Vol. 1, *The Dynamics of a City Church.* Chicago: University of Chicago Press, 1951.

The Notre Dame Study of Catholic Parish Life. Published as a series of fifteen reports from 1984 through 1989. Notre Dame, Ind. University of Notre Dame.

Nuesse, J., and T. Harte. *The Sociology of the Parish: An Introductory Symposium.* Milwaukee: Bruce, 1951.

1
Biblical Sources

The writings contained in the New Testament are the charter documents for the Roman Catholic Church as they are for all Christian churches. It is here that we begin our search for the authentic roots of parishes and other local communities of the faithful.

Jesus and the Jerusalem Church

After Jesus' resurrection, as he prepared to depart from this earth, he gave this charge to his followers: "You will receive power when the Holy Spirit comes upon you, and you will be my witnesses in Jerusalem, throughout Judea, and to the ends of the earth" (Acts 1:8). He instructed them to continue the mission he had begun.

Jesus had assured his disciples that "where two or three are gathered together in my name, there am I in the midst of them" (Mt 18:20). He chose his first disciples individually, calling them from their work to follow him. But the church, which con-   church
tinues the work of Christ in the world, consists not simply of individual Christians but of the followers of Christ *gathered into local communities.*

From its earliest appearances the church was a communion of communities. It existed as local congregations of the baptized, gathered together in communities and linked to other local congregations in other places in a network called "communion."

After Jesus' ascension and the coming of the Holy Spirit, the community of Jesus' followers in Jerusalem is described this way:

> They devoted themselves to the teaching of the apostles and to the communal life, to the breaking of the bread and to the prayers. (Acts 2:42)

The picture is of a close-knit group whose members cared for and were dependent on one another. They were intent on learning from those whom the Lord had chosen as his companions and witnesses. They commemorated the life, death and resurrection of Jesus at the eucharistic meal in their homes, and they devoted themselves to prayer in the temple. They lived in harmony and experienced remarkable growth.

> The community of believers was of one heart and mind...more than ever, believers in the Lord, great numbers of men and women, were added to them. (Acts 4:32 and 5:14)

Paul and His Churches

The letters of the apostle Paul bear the earliest witness to local Christian communities. They were written within two or three decades after the death of Jesus. They were addressed "to the church of the Thessalonians" (1 and 2 Thes 1:1), "to the church of God that is in Corinth" (1 and 2 Cor 1:1), "to all the beloved of God in Rome" (Rom 1:7), "to all the holy ones in Christ Jesus who are in Philippi, with the overseers and the ministers" (Phil 1:1).

Paul wrote to communities that he knew, some of which he personally founded and organized. He was aware of the internal life of those communities, and he addressed the problems and challenges that they were experiencing. His letters spoke of divisions, factions and conflicts within some churches. He even referred to instances of divorce, incest and profaning of the eucharist. He praised the communities for their faith, love, generosity, hospitality, courage and good works. Sin and grace both abounded in these early, human congregations.

Specific and concrete descriptions of those early communities are hard to come by. Even the population of some of the cities in which they were located is very difficult to estimate. The largest,

Rome, was home to nearly a million people in the first century. The smallest, some of the towns in what is now Turkey, were only a few thousand in population, some perhaps only a few hundred.

Within these cities and towns the "church" to which Paul wrote was made up of several "house churches" where the extended family and their friends met weekly for readings, reflection, prayer and the Lord's Supper. Paul refers to these household churches several times, for example, the church at the house of Prisca and Aquila (Rom 16:5; 1 Cor 16:19), the church at the house of Philemon (Phlm 2) and the church at the house of Nympha (Col 4:15).

These family-related groups, which assembled in homes, probably included not only parents and children but other relatives, slaves, former slaves and others connected to the family by trade or neighborhood. But these eucharistic assemblies were relatively small, limited to the number that could be accommodated in a dwelling, probably between fifteen and forty persons. These house churches have been called the basic cells of the Christian movement.

In addition to the house churches, some of the earliest Christian congregations resembled the kind of voluntary associations or social clubs (called *collegia* in Latin, *thiasoi* in Greek) that were quite common in the cities of the Greco-Roman world. Such associations were highly structured, quite stable and legally recognized. They were formed for three general purposes: commerce or profession (like guilds or trade associations), burial societies or religious worship. The religious associations (called *collegia sodalicia*) were devoted to the honor or cult of specific gods. Among them were some Jewish synagogues and Christian congregations.

The Jewish synagogues of the diaspora (those Jews scattered throughout the Greco-Roman world outside of Palestine) were another influence on the formation of early Christian communities. They were often the first places in which the itinerant missionaries (e.g., Paul, Barnabas, Timothy) began to preach, the first contact in a new city. And because many of the early Christians came from a Jewish background, the synagogue was a familiar social and religious structure on which to model an assembly of Christians.

Schools of philosophy, well known and respected in the cities of this period, provided still another social model for or influence on the Pauline communities. They often consisted of communities of disciples gathered around noted teachers of philosophy, rhetoric or ethics. Some of Paul's writing and preaching is very similar to the style of discourse used by these teachers. The modes of learning typical in these philosophic schools influenced the organization of instruction and exhortation in the early Christian communities.

The several small communities of Christians in each of the cities (e.g., Jerusalem, Antioch, Ephesus, Thessalonica, Corinth, Rome) would sometimes gather together in a common assembly, a meeting of "the whole church" (Rom 16:23; 1 Cor 14:23). This is the church to which Paul addressed his letters, that is, to the city-wide communion of small groups or house churches.

The churches of this first generation were far from uniform. They were diversely organized. Leaders had emerged, but patterns of leadership were not yet fixed. It was a time for founding and building communities. The householder served as host and patron for the house assemblies, for example, Stephanas in Corinth (1 Cor 16:15). Paul spoke of "those who labor among you and are over you in the Lord and admonish you" (1 Thes 5:12), thus naming three leadership roles or functions in that community. He later gave lists of leaders and functions (1 Cor 12:8, 28; Rom 12:6 and Eph 4:11). Although some patterns emerge from the lists (e.g., apostles, prophets, teachers, pastors or ministers), the names and functions are not the same. It is clear that at this time there was considerable variety and room for the emergence of individual leadership gifts within the communities.

These early communities were subject to God, to Christ, to the Spirit, to the scriptures and to the apostles, but they also possessed a large measure of freedom and autonomy. They were expected to make decisions for themselves, within the common ethos contained in the teaching they had received. They seemed to use a collegial mode for reaching agreement or consensus (e.g., see 1 Cor 5:4; Mt 18:17; Acts 15:4ff.). They received visits and letters from Paul and other evangelizers, but there was no trace of a hierarchical authority established over them.

The Next Generation

The churches portrayed in the later letters attributed to Paul, in the other New Testament letters (i.e., those of John, Peter, James and Jude), in Matthew's gospel and in the Book of Revelation represent another generation of local communities. They indicate the shape and life of local churches toward the end of the first century or the first part of the second.

The primary reality was still the community of believers. The members knew one another, related personally with each other (both well and ill) and prayed and celebrated and taught and learned together. The communities were far more significant than any leadership persons or groups within them, that is, their ministers.

By this time the communities had become stable and more structured. They had begun a process of institutionalization. A preoccupation with authentic teaching emerged, and with it a need to protect the communities against false teachers. This caused them to rely on official leaders as guarantors of authoritative teaching.

Three categories of official leaders appeared in the pastoral epistles (1 and 2 Timothy and Titus), although without the distinctions or clarity that they later attained. The three were named "elders," "overseers" and "ministers." The Greek words were *presbyteroi, episcopoi* and *diaconoi*. They later developed into the traditional titles: presbyters, bishops and deacons.

In the later books of the New Testament the elders and overseers, almost interchangeably, seemed to function as a community council of wise persons. They consisted of those who were seen to possess Christian depth and understanding. They were to be above reproach, married only once, hospitable, gentle, good managers of their own households, with their children under control, and not recent converts (1 Tm 3). These steady and respected leaders, selected from within the community, were to guide the group and assure that its faith was preserved and handed on sound and true.

It was by the appointment of these official ministers that the early churches sought to carry on after the death of the apostles. This development does not imply any lessening of the autonomy of the local communities. Each congregation was responsible for its life, its worship and its witness. At the same time, each was securely linked to all the others by the bonds of communion.

Those Who Belonged

What kind of people belonged to these earliest Christian communities? The first members were Jews, converts from Judaism. Sometime in the last half of the first century Gentiles became the majority. Ethnically, the communities were as diverse as the nations and regions where they were founded, a broad arc of cities across Asia Minor and the eastern Mediterranean from Jerusalem to Rome. Their membership included women, men and children of all those tribes and peoples.

The communities were heterogeneous in social class and economic standing. The churches were inclusive; they welcomed all who came to believe in Christ (illustrated by the acceptance of Gentiles, Acts 10–11 and 15, Gal 2). Only the very top and bottom of the social scale do not seem to have been represented. That is, the most powerful and the completely destitute are not encountered among those mentioned or alluded to in the New Testament sources. Nearly all other levels are mentioned: slaves and freed slaves, artisans, tradespeople, doctors, scribes, tentmakers, dealers in purple fabrics, relatively wealthy homeowners as well as those who "had not." The congregations reflected a cross section of urban society of the Greco-Roman world of the time. These followers of Christ were a tiny minority within each town or city.

The Concept of Communion

Communion expresses both the sharing of believers in Christ and the bond that links persons within Christian communities and the communities with one another. It is a profound expression of the union among Christians. The concept is based on the use of the Greek word *koinonia* in the New Testament, especially in the writings of Paul. The word means community, fellowship, or participation.

Paul spoke of our participation in Christ: "God is faithful, and by him you were called to fellowship with his Son, Jesus Christ, our Lord" (1 Cor 1:9). He also used the same expression for the fellowship at the Lord's Supper:

> The cup of blessing that we bless, is it not a participation in the blood of Christ? The bread that we break, is it not a participation in the body of Christ? (1 Cor 10:16)

The fellowship with Christ leads necessarily to the mutual fellowship of the members of the Christian community. This mutual recognition, acceptance, love and support were manifested in various ways, for example, the communal life of the Jerusalem community (Acts 2:42), agreement between apostles about their mission (Gal 2:9), contributions for the poor in Jerusalem (Rom 1:26) and the saving fellowship in which believers live (1 Jn 1:3, 7) and that the Holy Spirit strengthens (2 Cor 13:13).

Communion (*communio* in Latin) is a reciprocal religious relationship based on common faith and sacraments. It firmly and lovingly linked the earliest Christian communities together and was the basis for their communications and mutual assistance. The communities were conscious of being "in communion" with each other, and none of them broke communion with another.

The Word *Church*

The term chosen to name the reality embodied in the earliest Christian communities differed from the names given to other, similar entities of the time. The members of the communities, and the apostles and other missionaries who visited them and wrote to them, did not use the language of the Jewish synagogues, or of the social clubs or voluntary associations, or of the schools of philosophers. Instead they borrowed a specific term, the Greek word *ekklesia*, to name their Christian communities.

Ekklesia most commonly referred to the town meetings or voting assemblies of the free citizens of Greek and Roman cities.

This Greek word *ekklesia* had been used to translate the expression "assembly of God" or "those called together by God" *(qahal YHWH)* in the Hebrew scriptures when those scriptures were translated into Greek in Alexandria more than two centuries before Christ.

The Greek word *ekklesia* became *ecclesia* in Latin and is translated as *church* in English. It was used in the New Testament to name more than one kind of Christian community. The same term was employed for the small gatherings known as house churches, for the network of small groups in each city that Paul called "the whole church," for the churches of an entire region ("The church throughout all Judea, Galilee, and Samaria was at peace" [Acts 9:31]) and for the widespread Christian movement ("all who invoke the name of our Lord Jesus Christ in every place" [1 Cor 1:2]; see also 1 Cor 10:32; Mt 16:18). The single expression *church* referred to all four levels of reality: the smallest of local communities, the linked groups within a city, those of a larger region and the larger Christian movement.

Clearly, the word *church* was used analogously from the very beginning. It had several closely related meanings, which were not always easy to distinguish. But the most prevalent usage, and the one that was primary throughout the New Testament, referred to the local communities of Christians. *Church* first and foremost meant the gathering of the followers of Christ who lived and met in particular places, within definable geographical limits, for example, the church in Jerusalem, the church in Antioch, the church at Corinth.

(In the letters to the Colossians and Ephesians the word *church* was used in various idealized or spiritual senses, for example, as the body of Christ or as the spotless bride of Christ. These meanings convey great theological insight, but they do not refer immediately to the concrete congregations of Christians existing at the time.)

Sources and Readings

Brown, R. *The Churches the Apostles Left Behind.* New York: Paulist Press, 1984.

MacDonald, M. *The Pauline Churches.* Cambridge: Cambridge University Press, 1988.

Meeks, W. *The First Urban Christians: The Social World of the Apostle Paul.* New Haven: Yale University Press, 1983.

Osiek, C. *What Are They Saying about the Social Setting of the New Testament?* Mahwah, N.J.: Paulist Press, 1992.

Stambaugh, J., and D. Balch. *The New Testament in Its Social Environment.* Philadelphia: Westminster Press, 1986.

2
A History of Parishes

Introductory Notes

1. The history of the parish has not yet been written. There is no adequate, comprehensive history of Christian parishes. This is truly remarkable for a church that is essentially communal, that is, made up of local communities of believers. The story of the local congregations—their origins, size, activities, inner dynamics and how they responded to the religious needs of their members—has not yet been told.

By contrast, the leadership offices in the churches—the papacy, councils and synods, episcopacy, priesthood and diaconate—have been studied extensively. The chronicle of ordinary parishes through the centuries has been comparatively neglected.

What follows is an attempt to sketch an outline of the development of parishes by drawng upon the historical research that has been done.

2. It is important to bear in mind that in the first centuries of the church there was no single pattern of parish or diocesan organization, any more than there was a uniform pattern of ministerial offices. Nor was there a single trajectory or uniform path of development of church structures or offices. Variety and diversity abounded. East differed from West, rural from urban, France and Spain from Italy and North Africa. Developments took place at different times under different social and doctrinal pressures. The parish structures now familiar to us took a very long time to develop. It was not a smooth or simple historical chronology.

PAROIKIA

The Meaning of the Word *Parish*

Local Christian congregations began to be called "parishes" as *2nd century* early as the second century. The word first used was the Greek noun *paroikia,* which meant "those living near or beside." It had the sense of those people living in the same neighborhood. The verb form, *paroikein,* meant "to dwell beside." This was the primary meaning of the Greek word.

The Greek term also had a secondary meaning: "resident aliens, settled foreigners, nonnative sojourners." The word was used in the Greek versions of the Old and New Testament scriptures in this sense. It carried the meaning of persons in exile, like the Israelites in Egypt (Ex 2:22). It referred to aliens temporarily *Imp* residing in a foreign land, those who "have not here a lasting city, but seek the one that is to come" (Heb 13:14).

This secondary sense of the Greek word was the one first used by Christian writers for local congregations of believers. It was a *parish* spiritual or mystical notion that described the communities of those whose true homeland was in heaven, who were only pilgrims here on earth.

But soon *paroikia* came to mean individual churches living in the world. It became an accepted term for individual congregations within the larger church. It conveyed the sense of a people, a community, God's holy people (1 Pt 2:9–10).

Paroikia continued to name the local Christian communities in *4th century* the early centuries; by the fourth century it was used officially in church documents (e.g., in the acts of early church councils) for that purpose.

The church grew and spread rapidly in the fourth century after the Peace of Constantine (which began about 312). Latin joined Greek as an official language of the church. The local communities began to be described in Latin as *paroecia,* the translation of *paroikia.* This term had a less fixed and more fluid meaning. For a long time the Latin words *paroecia* and *dioecesis* were used somewhat interchangeably. That is, sometimes they referred to a local congregation led by a presbyter, and sometimes they referred to a cluster of local churches with a bishop at its head. Examples of this interchangeable usage can be found from the fourth century all the way to the thirteenth, even in official documents. *13th Century*

From the sixth century on, however, the terminology became more uniform, with the local congregations called parishes and the larger groupings of local churches within a territory and over-seen by a bishop called dioceses (or "eparchies" in the churches of the East).

The ecclesiastical terms *province, diocese* and *eparchy* all were administrative titles borrowed from the official language of the Roman Empire. *Parish,* by contrast, was simply a descriptive word for "those who live close to one another" or "sojourners in an alien land." But the original meaning of the word referred simply to people who dwell together.

Churches in Urban Centers

The earliest Christian communities formed in cities and towns rather than in the countryside. For example, within one hundred years after Jesus' death there were congregations in such cities as Jerusalem, Antioch, Corinth, Ephesus, Smyrna, Alexandria, Carthage, Lyons and Rome.

At first there was one community in each urban center, and it was headed by an overseer (*episkopos* in Greek, which we now trans-late as "bishop"). As these urban churches grew in size, there was need to meet in more than one location. The number of congre-gations in each city gradually increased, and communities formed in suburban or outlying areas as well. These subordinate "expan-sion" churches were usually headed by a presbyter (the word means "elder") deputed by the bishop. These presbyters formed an "order" or college that was advisory to the bishop and subject to him.

In the urban centers the communities began as domestic gath-erings or house churches. Their members came together at the home of one of them, usually one with a more spacious dwelling and courtyard, a space large enough for two or three score people to gather. In some cities, Rome and Antioch, for example, these house churches came to be known by the name of the host or patron who owned the home and welcomed the community to meet there. His or her name became the title of that house church, for example, "at Clement's."

As time went on and certain locations became associated with local congregations, they were named or titled after martyrs or other renowned Christians. Some of these buildings became dedicated to the uses of the community and came into the possession of the community. There were twenty such "titular churches" in Rome in the first half of the third century.

Each of the titular churches was served by a presbyter or two, and perhaps a deacon. They were quite consciously in communion with the bishop of the city or town. For example, they sometimes received the eucharistic bread *(fermentum)* sent to them from the bishop's own celebration of the Lord's Supper as a sign of that communion.

The titular churches were more personal than territorial, that is, they were not geographical subdivisions of the larger urban or regional church but simply congregations to which the faithful belonged. In other words, the titular churches of the third and fourth centuries were not parishes in our contemporary sense, but they were one of the forerunners of what later were called parishes.

Ever since the time of the titular churches Catholic parishes have borne the name of a saint or one of the titles of Christ or of the Blessed Virgin Mary. As late as the sixth century some rural parishes were simply named for their location, for example, "the church in the village of Riverton," but after that time all took the names of their patron saints.

Churches in Communion

The early urban congregations, although often quite distant from one another in the Mediterranean world, were quite conscious of being connected with one another. They felt joined together as parts of a larger organism. They had a sense of being "in communion" with one another.

Each congregation had its own compact unity, one carefully guarded against the dangers of factional divisons or false teachings. But the congregations knew that they did not exist in isolation. They were linked together in Christ as one people, one body, holding fast to the same faith and sharing in love. Their members were aware of having been baptized into Christ and into the larger church, the body of Christ, and they knew that they shared at the same table of the Lord even when at a distance.

Local churches welcomed those from other churches with hospitality. Congregations sent messages and received news from one another. They felt a sense of solidarity and responsibility for one another. This "catholicity" or consciousness of communion was present from the earliest times.

The Proliferation of Local Churches

Local churches began to mulitply and spread into villages of the countryside in the third century. This growth was the result of intense missionary activity and considerable periods of peace. These country subcongregations were entrusted to the care of a presbyter (rather than a bishop), sometimes one who was a traveling "circuit-rider" presbyter.

By the first quarter of the fourth century, when the final persecution of the church by the Emperor Diocletian ended, Christians were a substantial minority in the Roman Empire, roughly six or seven million persons out of a total population of about fifty million, according to one calculation. There were one hundred bishops, hundreds of local congregations, and numerous church buildings and other properties owned by them. Many church leaders had been killed in the persecution, many church buildings destroyed and property confiscated.

The period of peace and preferment that came with the Emperor Constantine, beginning in the year 312, was a major turning point in Christian history. From a status of suspicion, toleration and occasional outright persecution, the Christian congregations now enjoyed freedom, security and even favor. Confiscated property was restored, personal sanctions were lifted and bishops were given positions of prominence and influence. The emperor aided the church in many ways. For instance, he constructed splendid church buildings, the first in the basilica style (like official buildings or public markets), in Rome and in other cities of the empire.

This new situation occasioned a huge increase in church membership. Christianity became the majority religion in the Roman Empire within a hundred years of the Peace of Constantine. The church became a sort of "established church." In this climate of official preferment for the faith, many persons joined the church for opportunistic reasons. Their convictions and commitment were often quite shallow. Many were little more than nominal Christians. Formation in the faith was neglected in some places, even in the wake of vigorous missionary exertions.

Local churches multiplied under these new circumstances in the fourth and fifth centuries. These congregations formed in at least five different ways.

1. Most churches were still in cities and towns, authorized and governed by the bishop of the city. The bishop acted as spiritual leader, chief preacher and administrator of the property of the mother church, but at the same time he sent presbyters or deacons to give pastoral leadership to subsidiary congregations within the city.

2. Those faithful in hamlets and villages (*vici*) were cared for by itinerant pastors from the urban community, usually sent out by the urban bishop. Gradually, as the Christian population increased in the countryside, stable congregations were formed under the care of a permanently assigned presbyter or deacon. These churches grew in villages and market towns and along trade routes. In the East these parishes were often led by rural bishops called "cor-bishops" (*corepiskopoi*, "country bishops"). The leaders of these countryside parishes were subject to the bishop of the mother church in the city.

3. Monasteries were themselves small congregations, and monks offered pastoral care to those living within them as well as to those who worked on their lands or lived near the monasteries. Many parishes were primarily related to monastic communities, and some of the monks were ordained in order to give them leadership. (One bishop in Syria [about the year 450] reported that his diocese embraced eight hundred *paroikiai*. Perhaps he referred to rural districts or to small cells like "base communities." Most dioceses at the time would have had more like twenty to forty local congregations.)

In some outlying regions of the empire, for example, in

Ireland and Scotland, communities formed according to clans or around monasteries. Monks played a large part in the founding of rural parishes, often living in poverty among the laity and drawing people toward the faith by their preaching and example.

4. Some early parishes were also established as shrines or oratories over the burial places of saints or at sites associated with their activities. The saint, whose relics were in the church, became the patron of the place. The patron saint was the honored personality and symbol of the parish. In fact, juridically the parish property was considered to belong to the patron saint.

In a parallel way, churches were often built on the site of pagan temples, or the earlier temple was refashioned to the uses of Christian worship. This process was sometimes encouraged as a symbol of Christ's victory over darkness and evil.

5. Finally, owners of large estates *(villae)* sometimes built churches to serve the religious needs of those who lived on their lands. They would then either engage the services of a presbyter or seek one from the bishop of the nearest city.

All of these evolving forms of local parishes were related to the local bishop in some way, but the patterns were quite diverse. For example, the property of the local community sometimes belonged to the parish itself (Roman law permitted the local church to be a juridic person and own property in its own name), to the bishop, to the monastery, to the owner of the large estate or, indeed, to the patron saint of the parish! Things were far from settled or uniform.

Baptismal Churches

The baptism of new members was one of the functions reserved to the bishop in the early church. He was the regular minister of solemn baptism, and the authority to baptize was only gradually extended to other pastors.

House churches began to be fitted out with baptistries (a specific place or area for the bapstimal font) in the third century, or even earlier. The titular churches in Rome, which had become the property of the local congregation, were given the right to baptize new members on their own premises rather than use private bathhouses or the Tiber River for that purpose.

When local congregations spread out from the cities into the hinterland in the fourth and fifth centuries, the right to baptize persons within a specified area was one of the ways in which major churches were distinguished from lesser churches and oratories.

Baptismal churches *(ecclesiae baptismales)* were those churches that possessed a baptistry and where baptisms were administered. They were the more important churches, found in principal locations, and their territory was extensive. Often they were headed by an archpresbyter (the *arch* meant "chief" or "ranking"). The baptismal churches were analogous to the churches headed by the bishops in the cities, and they became the characteristic feature of a system of parishes that began to develop in the sixth century. This evolution marked a process of decentralization within dioceses.

Interestingly, a baptismal church was sometimes called *plebs,* the people's church, and the presbyter who headed it was referred to as a *plebanus,* or people's priest.

This pattern of baptismal churches prevailed in rural areas of France and Spain, parts of Italy, Germany, Scandinavia and England throughout the early Middle Ages. Lesser churches in these regions, such as shrines, private oratories and monastery chapels, were subordinated to the baptismal churches. These were not permitted to celebrate baptisms or to have the eucharist on major feasts, when the faithful were obliged to attend the local baptismal church. The baptismal churches acquired a degree of autonomy and were often served by several presbyters living together in a small community, much like the bishops' churches in the cities.

The forming of new Christians in the catechumenate (to the extent that it was still done)—their ritual entry into full communion and their further formation in faith and witness—was appropriately used as a distinguishing characteristic of a full-fledged parish in this system of baptismal churches.

The large baptismal churches evolved into deaneries in the

ninth and tenth centuries. That is, they became clusters of parishes in distinct regions of the diocese headed by a dean who assisted the bishop in administration of the congregations in that area.

Proprietary Churches

The descriptive term *proprietary churches* meant that the churches were actually privately owned, that is, the buildings were the property of the local landlord, the prince or feudal lord who owned the land. The landowner treated the churches as his personal possessions. He could sell them or bequeath them to his heirs, and he could hire and fire the presbyter who had pastoral care of the people.

The development of proprietary churches had profound and lasting effects on local congregations in the Catholic tradition. Proprietary churches (from the German *Eigenkirchen*, literally "own churches") were a product of the feudal system in Europe, which began in the eighth century. They grew out of Germanic law rather than from the Roman law system, which declined in influence as the Roman Empire broke up.

Germanic law developed in an agrarian society, and its values were closely related to the land. Nearly everything was viewed in terms of the land, interests in land and income from the land. In contrast to Roman law, there was no concept of public law or public administration.

The local church was literally tied to the land; the stone altar was built into the ground. The church building, churchyard, cemetery, parish house, garden, fields and orchards all were of a piece, all part of the property of the estate, and the property belonged to the landowner.

The feudal system was based on the agreement of vassalage in which subordinates pledged their homage, fealty and service to a local lord in exchange for his protection and the use of some land or other source of income. The local presbyter was viewed as one of the vassals, and part of the income from the church and its lands was his support, in addition to the stole fees for sacramental administration and the free-will offerings of the faithful. But he was appointed by and answerable to the landowner, who may have had slight regard for his ministerial abilities.

This private church system became so pervasive after the eighth century that it extended to nearly every church in central and northern Europe, including baptismal churches, monasteries and even cathedrals. Their properties were often treated as private possessions by local rulers, and their leaders (pastors, abbots, even bishops) were named by the local lord. Often they appointed relatives and friends to such positions. The one appointed had to be loyal to the lord and render to him a share of the revenue from the property. This radical privatization of church property and pastoral offices impoverished the church spiritually, and often financially.

The church struggled for centuries to free its local congregations from the bondage of this privatized system. Charlemagne, the king of the Franks (from 786 to 814) and emperor of the Holy Roman Empire (after 800), ordered control of the local churches returned to the bishops. Although church property remained in the hands of the landholders, the bishops at least regained supervision of divine services and the maintenance of the churches, as well as the right to approve the appointment of clergy. Since such appointments were permanent, the local presbyter could not be removed by either the landlord or the bishop, except after judgment of a church court. Hence, the presbyter became more independent of both the owner and the bishop, though he was clearly subordinate to the bishop and reported to him.

The church's struggle to be freed from this form of domination by secular powers continued until the Gregorian Reform (1049–1122). It was known as the Investiture Controversy because the appointments were made by the ceremonial investing of the clerics with the symbols of office (e.g., book, staff, stole, etc.). Even after the bishops' approval of such appointments was recovered, civil rulers and landlords exercised great influence over ecclesiastical appointments well into the late Middle Ages.

The Benefice System

As a result of the proprietary church structures, a great inversion occurred in the way that local congregations were officially viewed. Legally, parishes became characterized as pastoral offices that provided support for the clergy rather than communities for the spiritual welfare of the faithful.

It seems almost incredible in retrospect, but for several centuries parishes were defined as benefices. A benefice is a sacred office, like that of pastor, to which is connected the permanent right to receive income from the endowment attached to the office. In the church's juridical order, from the twelfth century until the Code revision of 1983, a parish was looked upon as a spiritual reality (the pastoral office) with a temporal reality (the endowment or other income source) united in one institution: a benefice, that is, an office with a reliable income source for the officeholder.

The benefice system evolved out of the proprietary churches. Actual ownership of church property was gradually returned to church authorities, but the former owners remained as patrons, that is, they retained the right to present the officeholder, the pastor of the parish. The bishop could accept or reject the person presented, but once approved and installed the person became the beneficiary, the one who enjoyed a lifetime income from the benefice.

The benefice system, as strangely privatized as it may seem, accomplished three valuable ends: it restored episcopal control over pastoral appointments, it provided support for the parish clergy and it safeguarded church property. The beneficiary (parish pastor) had the right only to the income from the benefice. He could not sell or otherwise dispose of the property; especially he could not leave it to his heirs. (Rural clergy were more often than not married and, naturally enough, desired to give an inheritance to their children.)

The life of the parish community was not greatly affected by this way of characterizing the parish as a benefice. The canonical focus seemed to be on the office, officeholder and his endowed income, but spiritual and sacramental care continued as before. Pastoral care was not at a high level. Both clergy and people were

poorly educated, if at all, and the pastors were often barely liter-
ate. Their ability to preach and administer sacraments was minimal. Still, parish life went on: children were baptized, mass
celebrated, some instruction given, sinners reconciled, marriages
witnessed, the sick visited and the dead buried.

Collegiate Churches in the Cities

Cathedral churches in the cities, from as early as the fifth century, were served by several presbyters rather than by a single pastor. They were appointed by and under the supervision of the
local bishop. These clerics often lived in common, like monks in a
monastery. They shared together in the ministry of the cathedral,
its liturgical services and its pastoral duties.

As time went on, other larger churches were served by similar
"colleges" (from the Latin *collegium*, persons united in the same
office or calling) of clerics. At first they were all "seculars," the
bishop's presbyters, but later they also included "regulars," those
who followed a monastic rule (*regula* in Latin), as well as monks
themselves. In each case, they exercised the pastoral care for a
local congregation together, jointly, as a college, with shared
responsibilities for various facets of the ministry. These churches
were called "collegiate churches."

In the eleventh and twelfth centuries these collegiate churches
were also structured juridically and financially as benefices. Each
member of the college who shared in the spiritual office of pastoral care for the local church was entitled to a share of the
income from the endowment. There was a regular distribution of
these shares (or *prebends*) to the members of the college as a sort
of salary. This continued long after the clerics ceased the practice
of living a common life.

These collegiate parishes in urban areas often received a better
level of pastoral care since they had larger resources and attracted
more educated clergy, sometimes the younger children of noble
families.

The thirteenth century saw the rise and spread of the mendicant
religious communities, such as the Franciscans, Dominicans and
Carmelites. They engaged in itinerant preaching and teaching,

but when they founded their convents in cities and towns, they attracted people who were nourished by their preaching. (Often the mendicants were better educated and preached more effectively than their secular counterparts.) The churches related to these religious houses multiplied throughout the cities of Europe in the thirteenth and fourteenth centuries and remained a permanent feature of urban congregational life.

Parish Life and Church Reform

At critical moments in the long life of the Catholic Church, reformers have made strenuous efforts to renew and purify the church, to call it back to its original mission and authentic life. Often the renewal of parish life has been at the heart of these reform movements. Three examples stand out.

1. Charlemagne and those who followed him as emperors of the Holy Roman Empire (in what is known as the Carolingian Reform, roughly from 750 to 900) worked hard at reforming and stabilizing the church as well as unifying their empire. One of their reforming principles was to establish a church, its endowment and a priest in every village. To a remarkable extent they succeeded, and the system of parishes that they set up endured for centuries in western Europe, through the darkest times of feudal disruption and chaos.

Urged by royal mandate, a local landowner would build a church on his estate, endow it with some arable land and the tithes from the people served by the church and appoint a pastor. If the church had parish status, the pastor had to be approved by the bishop, and the bishop exercised governance over the pastoral ministrations performed by the priest. This parish arrangement was based on the delicately balanced cooperation of both secular and religious authorities, in keeping with the economic system of the period. The landowners were motivated by a desire to have Christian teaching and worship close at hand for themselves and their people.

2. The Fourth Lateran Council, the greatest of medieval councils, took place in Rome in 1215. It was called by Pope Innocent III (1198–1216) and was one of his powerful attempts to bring

order, freedom and reform to the church. It included provisions
for parish life that are part of the church's discipline to this day.
For example, the council enjoined every Christian to annual confession, to Easter communion and to the observance of marriage
regulations. It called for better preaching, pastoral care of the
sick, improved education for those to be ordained priests, moral
integrity in those placed in charge of churches, observance of
clerical celibacy and sobriety, and a regular visitation of every
parish by the diocesan bishop. The council forbade anyone to
have more than one benefice that involves the care of souls. This
series of reform decrees indicates the presence of abuses at the
parish level at the time, but it also shows an awareness of the
importance of a sound parish life, a healthy and nourishing relationship between the people and their pastor.

3. The Council of Trent (1545–1563) was the keystone of
the Catholic Counter-Reform in reaction to the Protestant
Reformation. One of its profound achievements was the renewal
of pastoral care at the parish level. The council made preaching
and catechetical instruction on every Sunday and holy day an
obligation for parish priests, and also required them to provide
sacramental and moral education for their people. It insisted that
pastors maintain residence in the parish entrusted to them.
Bishops were asked "for the spiritual good of souls" to assign the
faithful within their dioceses to clear and distinct parishes so that
all the people will have pastors who will know them and from
whom they may receive the sacraments. This was to be done as
soon as possible (session 24, canon 13). When parishes became
vacant, bishops were to appoint promptly as new pastors those
who were found to be the most worthy, based on a system of
examinations.

The council clarified and proclaimed Catholic faith in many
areas. It especially emphasized the sacramental life. It encouraged the devout reception of the sacraments and strove to eliminate mistaken impressions or superstitious practices regarding
them. As a result, eucharistic piety (e.g., benediction, proces-
sions) greatly increased in parishes. Also Marian devotions, such
as the rosary, became a staple of Catholic life.

It was a long while before the decrees of the Council of Trent took effect throughout the church, but they eventually brought about more uniform patterns of parish life. They eliminated the historical differences between urban and rural parishes and moved strongly in the direction of territorial parishes (as over against personal parishes). Unfortunately the Tridentine Reform stressed hierarchical authority and clerical leadership to such an extent that it left the lay members of the church in a purely passive role.

All three of these very different reform movements, in the ninth, thirteenth and sixteenth centuries, focused on the life of the local community of faith. They strove to remedy neglect, misconduct and various forms of corruption (mostly, but not exclusively, clerical), and they stressed the central importance of pastoral care.

> All to whom care of souls has been entrusted are subject to the divine command to know their sheep (Jn 10:1–16), to offer sacrifice for them, to nourish them by preaching God's word, by administering the sacraments and by the example of good works of every kind, to have fatherly care of the poor and of all others who are wretched, and to be devoted to other pastoral duties. (Council of Trent, session 23, canon 1)

The reformists were concerned about many other matters, such as correct doctrine and political pressures, but they were always conscious that what really mattered was the life of the local congregations of the faithful.

The Missions

The sixteenth century, in addition to being the scene of the Protestant Reformation and the Catholic Counter-Reform, witnessed the greatest missionary exertion in history. Whole new worlds were discovered by Spanish and Portuguese explorers, and the missionaries were right beside them, attempting to bring Christ to the people of these strange and exotic lands.

Both religious and secular priests accompanied the explorers (and exploiters) who found and developed the New World for their respective countries, but the Dominicans, Franciscans,

Carmelites, Augustinians and Jesuits distinguished themselves in this great missionary effort. It began with the Franciscans in the Antilles (what is now the Dominican Republic, Haiti, Cuba and Puerto Rico) in 1500, just a few years after Columbus' discovery. The Spanish missionaries then proceeded to Mexico, Peru, Panama, Paraguay, Bolivia, Chile, Venezuela, Argentina and the Philippines before the end of the century.

The Portuguese struggled to evangelize Brazil, West Africa, the Congo, Angola, East Africa, India, Goa, Japan, China and Indochina, with vastly different success, all within this same century.

These mission communities took various forms and certainly could not at first be described as parishes. They were groups of newly baptized people in ports and outposts, village stations and rural areas, where the missionaries built chapels, schools, clinics and their own monastic dwellings. Often the missionaries were circuit riders, making long treks from one settlement to another, preaching and administering the sacraments as they went.

There were severe impediments to the authentic development of indigenous local churches. The heart of the missionary work was seen to be preaching the gospel and baptizing those who responded. Beyond that, the only sacraments stressed were confession and matrimony. For decades the natives were not allowed communion. For the entire century no natives were ordained to the priesthood. Little attempt was made to adapt the western European religious forms to these very different cultures. A measure of colonizing was mixed in with the Christianizing of all these native peoples.

Despite these radical handicaps, the missions thrived and grew in many areas. As these young churches set down roots and became stable institutions as well as congregations of persons, they took on the shapes and styles of western European parishes for the most part. The missionaries helped the natives toward forms of church life that they themselves had known. The mission churches gradually became settled parishes in the cities and villages of the New World.

The herculean missionary effort of the sixteenth century produced new Christian territories and millions of baptized persons, but, more importantly, it resulted in thousands of new local Christian communities.

The Modern State and the Industrial Revolution

Two major developments in the eighteenth and nineteenth centuries powerfully influenced Catholic parish life. One was the emergence of the modern absolutist states, which used the church for their own purposes, and the other was the industrial revolution, which caused huge population shifts and overwhelmed traditional parishes as communities of people and structures of pastoral care.

The development of strong central governments in what is now Spain, Germany, Austria, France, Belgium, Italy, Poland and most of Latin America began at different times and progressed in different modes, but it had profound effects on the church. It is somewhat simplistic to generalize because the historical experiences were so different. Some of the effects resulted from revolution and violent persecution of the church, others from imperial authority determined to place the church at the service of the common good. However, some parallels emerged.

There was a pattern of large-scale appropriation of church properties, sometimes called "secularization," by the governments. Property owned by the church had become very extensive; in France, for example, it was estimated to amount to one-third of the entire country. The governments strictly regulated the remaining property as well as the activities of the church and its ministers. There resulted a form of established church or official recognition of the church by the state, which had mixed consequences.

Eventually, there was a sort of compensation for the confiscated property in the form of state support for the parish clergy and the restoration and maintenance of parish buildings. But even these forms of compensation came with a cost: often the state set the boundaries and conditions for parishes as well as dioceses, and the clergy tended to assume the attitudes associated with civil servants rather than those of ministers of the church.

The second major development that influenced the church at

the level of its local communities was the industrial revolution (roughly from 1750 to 1900). With the invention of modern means of transportation, communications and industrial production came the concentration of resources and employment in cities. People migrated from rural to urban areas in vast numbers. The number of cities with large populations (e.g., more than one hundred thousand) grew exponentially, from a mere handful in 1750 to more than seven hundred by 1950.

The model of the territorial parish, which was based on natural communities of those who lived near one another in stable and clearly defined neighborhood areas, was simply overwhelmed by this new urban situation of teeming apartment complexes and highly mobile populations. By 1900 the average parish in the city of Paris contained 40,000 people. In Buenos Aires the average was more than 50,000 by 1910. A parish in Milan that had 1,600 people in 1800 by 1900 counted 43,000. The city of Essen grew from 6,000 people in 1850 to more than 200,000 by 1890, when it still had only two parishes.

The delivery of basic pastoral care (e.g., baptisms, eucharistic celebrations, marriages, funerals) had become nearly impossible in these new circumstances. The formation of real parish communities, where people who knew one another shared their faith and worship, was simply out of the question.

The American Experience of Parish

In 1785 the Catholic population of the United States was no more than 25,000 (almost all in Maryland and Pennsylvania) out of a total of four million. By 1815 it had grown to about 150,000 and was served by one hundred priests. The number more than quadrupled to 660,000 by 1840. However, thanks to the Irish and German immigrations, the number of Catholics increased to 4.5 million by 1870, 11 percent of the total population. Three thousand priests ministered to them.

This new and growing church was able to find its own identity and style in a country committed to religious liberty. Catholics thrived as a nonestablished church, with no state support but where the free exercise of religion was constitutionally assured.

More concretely, the church in the United States was free of any governmental involvement in appointments to church offices and free from the rights of patrons in the benefice system to make presentation of candidates for pastors of parishes. Local congregations could form themselves or be established by bishops without any outside interference, but they existed as minority groups within a dominantly Protestant culture.

In the early years, before and after the colonies declared and won their independence as a nation, the Catholic status was missionary. They gathered in homes or farms, trading posts or forts, or at country chapels whenever a traveling missionary priest stopped by. There were only a few parishes before 1810, and most of those were in eastern cities like Boston, New York, Philadelphia, Baltimore and Charleston.

Those early parishes were often founded and organized by the laity. Because of the shortage of priests and the widely dispersed population, groups of laypersons took the initiative in many parish activities. They would meet together, collect funds, find property or a place to meet, and request a priest from the bishop or try to entice one to come over from Europe. When they had a priest, they would continue to govern the parish along with the priest by means of elected lay trustees. The trustees (perhaps six or eight of them) were elected each year from among those who rented pews, that is, those men who had some resources and were committed members of the parish. They exercised control over the temporal affairs of the parish and participated in the selection of their pastors.

This system of lay trustees, although it occasioned conflicts from time to time, was the normative form of parish government in the early years, and it was well accepted by the bishops. At first, there was no other way for a parish to hold property under state laws. Later, the immigrants who bought and paid for their churches insisted on having some say in the way they were run.

Laypersons also took on many other responsibilities in the parish besides the financial and administrative; for example, they led the community in prayer when there was no priest and taught catechism to the children.

The number of Catholic parishes grew dramatically, especially because of the large groups of Catholic immigrants that arrived during the nineteenth century. Irish, German, Italian, Polish and French people came in great numbers, in addition to the many Mexicans who were annexed or who migrated to the United States. The Catholic population increased from 195,000 in 1820 to 3,100,000 in 1860; the number of churches grew from 124 to 2,385 in that same time.

While most of the parishes were founded by priests under the direction of the diocesan bishop, many were formed through lay initiative. A number successfully retained a lay trustee form of governance.

The American bishops repeatedly insisted, from 1829 to 1884, that parish property be held, not by the lay trustees, but by the diocese (it was usually in the name of the bishop). In the national council of 1884 they finally secured that goal, but at the same time they encouraged lay participation in the governance of local churches. The conciliar legislation provided for elected parish committees or trustees and spelled out the qualifications for candidates.

"National parishes" proved to be very effective structures for the Catholic immigrant communities. National parishes, or "personal parishes," are those that are organized for language or ethnic groups rather than on a territorial basis. Nearly every immigrant group, in all parts of the country, whether by its own initiative or that of the local bishop, was accommodated by this means. The people were able to worship in their own tongue, sing familiar hymns, carry on their particular devotions and customs and have a priest who could assist them in doing so. The pattern of national parishes was integral to the upbuilding of the Catholic Church in the United States, as it was to the integration of many immigrant peoples into American culture.

Several of the immigrant groups, notably the Germans, French, Polish, Slovaks, Ukrainians and Lithuanians, felt very strongly about the ownership and control of their parish properties. They were generous in contributing to the acquisition and development of their churches, and they wished to retain title to the real estate as well as to have some say in the direction of the parishes. This late-nineteenth and early-twentieth century phenomenon paralleled the earlier pattern of lay trustee involvement and occasioned some of the same conflicts with bishops. In at least two instances, the Polish National Church and the Ukrainian Ruthenians, the conflicts resulted in schisms within the U.S. church.

The Catholic Church in the United States continued to experience remarkable growth (16.4 million by 1910) and strength, even after the major waves of immigration subsided. Parishes multiplied (16,000 churches by 1920), following the growth and movement of the general population. As a result of policies adopted at the 1884 national council, Catholic schools became an important component of most parishes (there were nearly 5,000 schools by 1910). "First the school, then the church" was the motto.

The vitality of Catholic parish life by the mid-twentieth century was impressive. Vocations to the priesthood and religious life were plentiful, and Catholics were moving up the socioeconomic ladder. Some parish plants—church, rectory, convent, school(s), hall, playground–parking lot, etc.—were massive, expensive and functional. Many parishes were vibrant centers of neighborhood life. Parish-based organizations (e.g., Altar and Rosary, Holy Name, St. Vincent de Paul) were large and active.

After the Second Vatican Council, the number of candidates for the priesthood and religious life began to drop. The decrease has been precipitous, and it has not stopped. At the same time, the Catholic laity continues to increase in levels of education and affluence and in sheer numbers. These two factors, together with the sense of lay empowerment that followed from the theology of the council, have caused dramatic changes in American Catholic parishes.

Parishes are served by many fewer priests, while their staffs of lay and religious ministers have burgeoned, and increasing numbers of parishes and missions are led by laypersons. Lay involvement in all parish activities has reached a level not seen since the lay leadership of the early years of the American democracy. Parishes in inner cities and national parishes are being merged, clustered or closed in many cities, although the total number of parishes remains nearly the same (just under twenty thousand nationally for a Catholic population that is approaching sixty million). Thousands of parish schools have closed.

Parish Activities

What do parishes do? Looking back over this brief historical sketch of local congregations of Christian believers, what are the patterns of activity that are typical and common to them? They fall into four general categories:

1. Proclamation and formation: preaching the word of God, handing on the tradition and educating the members of the community in faith and Christian living, through catechetical programs, sacramental instructions and schools.

2. Worship and sacramental celebrations: baptism and confirmation of new members, Sunday eucharists, reconciliation of penitents, marriages, anointing of the sick, burial of the dead, prayer, devotions and missions.

3. Works of charity and care: looking after orphans and widows, providing for the hungry, homeless and unemployed, helping to settle new immigrants and upbuilding the community.

4. Outreach and social concerns: evangelizing the unchurched and reconciling the alienated; and cooperating with others in solidarity of witness and endeavor against war and violence, for justice and peace, against ignorance and disease, and for human and environmental development.

The categories of congregational activity are stated in contemporary terms, but their counterparts can be traced in history. Not all these activities were present in every age, and some were performed minimally, even dismally, at times, superbly at others. They are the "vital signs" that indicate the state of the local Catholic community—healthy and thriving or failing and moribund—whether in first-century Jerusalem or in twenty-first-century Chicago.

Sources and Readings

Bernier, P. *Ministry in the Church: A Historical and Pastoral Approach.* Mystic, Conn.: Twenty-Third Publications, 1992.

Blochlinger, A. *The Modern Parish Community.* New York: P.J. Kenedy & Sons, 1965.

Dolan, J. *The American Catholic Experience: A History from Colonial Times to the Present.* New York: Doubleday, 1985.

————, ed. *The American Catholic Parish: A History from 1850 to the Present,* 2 vols. New York: Paulist Press, 1987.

Floristan, C. *The Parish—Eucharistic Community.* Notre Dame, Ind.: Fides, 1964.

Hennesey, J. *American Catholics: A History of the Roman Catholic Community in the United States.* New York: Oxford University Press, 1981.

Jedin, H., and J. Dolan, eds. *History of the Church,* 10 vols. New York: Herder & Herder and Crossroad, 1965–1981.

Jungmann, J. *The Early Liturgy to the time of Gregory the Great.* Notre Dame, Ind.: University of Notre Dame Press, 1959.

3
A Theology of
the Local Church

Theology is faith seeking understanding. Christians believe many things. They believe in God, in Jesus Christ, in the Holy Spirit, in grace, in salvation and in the church. They take these things on faith, with gratitude to God for the gift of faith. Since its beginning the Christian community has desired to understand its beliefs, to see them more clearly, to plumb them more deeply, to grasp them more firmly. Members of the church have searched the scriptures and the long Christian tradition for that further understanding. They have looked for perceptions, insights, explanations and some greater synthesis so that they can better appreciate and cherish their faith. For these reasons this chapter is devoted to an attempt to articulate a theology of the local church.

The church itself became an object of theological reflection relatively late in its history. It was in 1300 that the first theological treatise explicitly on the church was published, *De Ecclesia* by James of Viterbo. That work, and nearly all of subsequent "ecclesiology" or theology of the church, was concerned with the universal church, the pope, the bishops and the power and authority that the church received from Christ.

Only quite recently, actually in the twentieth century, has there been a sustained theological reflection on the local church, that is to say, on the congregations of baptized persons gathered in specific places.

41

This development of a theology of the local church grew out of five different movements within the larger world of Catholic theology during this century: (1) biblical, the reexamination of the churches of the New Testament, (2) patristic, the renewed study of the earliest Christian writers and their churches, (3) liturgical, the renewal of the church's worship and sacramental life, (4) missionary, the rediscovery of the proclamation of God's word to the unchurched and (5) ecumenical, the appreciation of and dialogue with other Christian churches. These five movements, which called forth intense research, study and reflection, were like five strands with which Catholic theology wove a new, strong fabric to support a richer and fuller understanding of its basic communities of faith.

Now there is a theology of the local church, and it bears the authoritative stamp of the Second Vatican Council. It may help to explore the maturation of this theology before, during, and since the council. (To be clear, the expression *local church* is used here in the sense of parish or other small community of the Catholic faithful, not, as it is sometimes used, in the sense of diocese, that grouping of churches headed by a bishop.)

Before the Second Vatican Council

One expression of a theology of the local church envisioned it as a miniature of the universal church. It was called "a little church within the church" (*ecclesiola in ecclesia*). The parish was a cell of the larger church, like one of the cells of the human body, which contains the same genetic material, a microcosm.

The local church was seen as a tiny version of the universal church, the whole church writ small. In other words, the theology of the church universal was projected down upon the local congregation. It was seen as a miniature of the mystical body of Christ.

Another image used of the local church was that of the family: the parish is to the world church as the family is to the society, namely its basic structural unit.

The advantage of this view of the local church as a miniature was that it used a theological starting point. The local church was seen from a theological perspective rather than from a sociological or juridical (canonical) standpoint. But this theology ran into problems when it carried the comparison too far. It compared the pastor of the parish to Christ himself and suggested that the pastor was the head of the local "mystical body" and the source of all grace for the entire community! In this case then, what is true of the whole (the church universal) is not true in every respect of the part (the individual parish).

Yves Congar, the great French Dominican theologian, used the family metaphor for the local church in a different way. He compared the parish to a family household and the diocese to the town or city within which it existed. Christians are born and nurtured in their own local church just as they are born and raised as human persons within their family. But there is need for a larger, more complete and complementary context for human life to be fully developed (the neighborhood, town or city), and that larger life for Christians is the diocese, with its greater variety and resources.

The local church is the embodiment of the larger church, its specific geographic location and set of human conditions. Just as human beings are born into specific families in concrete locations and conditions, so Christians are baptized and formed in Christ in specific local churches. These gatherings together in communion with the Lord have value in their own right. That is, they are not means to a larger end, but they themselves are realizations of the church.

These local embodiments or realizations build the church up from below. They are connected with the larger church through the hierarchical presence and appointment of their pastor, but in themselves they are God's holy people (the *plebs sancta*), a community that includes both priest and people. (In large urban parishes, much too large to form real communities, there can be within them several smaller communities based on neighborhood, ethnic group, employment, interests or concerns.) The parish, Congar wrote, should be a community of prayer, spiritual life, mutual service and apostolic activity; it should be a liturgical, caring, missionary community.

Karl Rahner, the eminent German Jesuit theologian, described the parish as the local actualization of the church. The church is a visible society that reaches a higher degree of actuality (than merely continuing in existence) when it becomes an actual event perceptible in space and time, an event as the communion of saints. In the celebration of the eucharist the local church is most intensely event because the union of the faithful with Christ and with each other is realized visibly and intimately.

The starting point for a theology of the parish, Rahner thought, is this local materialization of the church, not its derivation from higher jurisdictions as territorial parts or divisions. That is the reason why individual communities were called churches in the New Testament. They are the primary realizations of the church as an event. The parish is the primary, normal and original form of the local Christian community because of the principle of locality: a union of people who live together as neighbors in the same place.

Each local church, according to Rahner, is a manifestation of the whole church, making it tangible, enabling it to realize its "historical place-time apprehensibility."

Other theologians writing before the council spoke of the parish as the image of the universal church, the very representation and achievement of the church, the first and most profound ecclesial community of sacrifice, prayer and life. One called the parish "the first community of Christian life in the Church of Jesus Christ." It was described as "the primary and essential center of ecclesial life, and a missionary community."

Another wrote: "The parish community is the Holy Church, the people of God, the salvific community of the Messiah, the family of the baptized living in one specific area, in the midst of the human community." The parish community is the bearer of salvation for all those who make up the larger human community. It is a public manifestation of God's love for them, and consequently it bears serious responsibilities.

The Teaching of the Council

The Second Vatican Council (1962–1965), one of the great events in the entire history of the church, resoundingly affirmed the reality of the local church. The council's first major teaching document, the *Constitution on the Sacred Liturgy,* urged the promotion of the liturgy in lesser (than the diocese) groupings of the faithful:

> Among these, parishes set up locally under a pastor who takes the place of the bishop are the most important: for in a certain way they represent the visible Church as it is established throughout the world.
>
> Therefore the liturgical life of the parish and its relationship to the bishop must be fostered in the thinking and practice of both laity and clergy; efforts must also be made to encourage a sense of community within the parish, above all in the common celebration of the Sunday Mass. (*SC* 42)

Parishes "re-present," make present, the worldwide church. They realize it (make it real) especially when the congregation with its pastor celebrates the eucharist on Sunday.

The *Dogmatic Constitution on the Church,* the council's central theological document, spoke of the presence of Christ and the church in each local community:

> This church of Christ is truly present *(vere adest)* in all legitimate local congregations of the faithful, which united with their pastors, are themselves called churches in the New Testament. For in their own locality these are the new people called by God, in the Holy Spirit in much fullness (1 Thes 1:5). In them the faithful are gathered together by the preaching of the gospel of Christ, and the mystery of the Lord's Supper is celebrated, "so that the whole fellowship is joined together through the flesh and blood of the Lord's body" (Mozarabic prayer).
>
> In these communities, though frequently small and poor, or living far from each other, Christ is present. By His power the one, holy, catholic and apostolic church is gathered together. (*LG* 26)

This passage refers explicitly to parishes and other local communities of worship within the diocese. In each one of them Christ is present in the word and the sacrament and the fellowship. Each one is church in the true sense of the word, just as the local communities named in the New Testament were.

This solemn teaching of the council shows that an authentic theology of the church can start with the concrete community,

church

the local church, where the word of God is preached and the saving death of Jesus is proclaimed in the eucharist.

The council's *Decree on the Church's Missionary Activity* describes
the formation of local churches as the work of the Holy Spirit who
in baptism "begets to a new life those who believe in Christ [and]
gathers them into the one People of God...." Missionaries, as
God's co-workers, are to

> raise up congregations of the faithful who will walk in a manner
> worthy of the vocation to which they have been called (Eph 4:1),
> and will exercise the priestly, prophetic and royal office which God
> has entrusted to them. In this way, the Christian community
> becomes a sign of God's presence in the world. For by reason of
> the Eucharistic Sacrifice, this community is ceaselessly on the way
> with Christ to the Father. Carefully nourished on the word of God,
> it bears witness to Christ. And, finally, it walks in love and glows
> with an apostolic spirit. (*AG* 15)

The decree describes these local Christian communities as deeply
rooted in their own cultures, in dialogue with the societies
around them and ecumenically cooperative with other Christian
groups.

The council went on to treat various aspects of life and ministry
in parishes, for example: *Dogmatic Constitution on the Church* (*LG*
28), *Decree on the Bishop's Pastoral Office* (*CD* 30–32), *Constitution on
the Liturgy* (*SC* 10–11, 14, 26–30) and the *Decree on the Apostolate of
the Laity* (*AA* 10, 18, 25, 30). The council did not, however, further
develop the theology of the local church itself.

Developments Since the Council

Thirty years have passed since the Second Vatican Council
closed. Official Catholic teaching has restated and emphasized the
council's theology of the local church. Pope John Paul II's
Apostolic Exhortation on the Laity (Christifideles Laici), which followed
the 1987 Synod on the Laity, offers one salient example:

> The ecclesial community, while always having a universal dimen-
> sion, finds its most immediate and visible expression in the
> parish. It is there that the church is seen locally. It is necessary that

in the light of faith all rediscover the true meaning of the parish, that is, the place where the very "mystery" of the church is present and at work....The parish is not principally a structure, a territory or a building, but rather "the family of God, a fellowship afire with a unifying spirit," "a familial and welcoming home," the "community of the faithful." Plainly and simply, the parish is founded on a theological reality, because it is a eucharistic community. This means that the parish is a community properly suited for celebrating the eucharist, the living source for its upbuilding and the sacramental bond of its being in full communion with the whole church. (*CL* 26)

Catholic theologians who study the church have continued to reflect on and explore the nature of the local church and its relationship to the larger church, that is, the diocese and universal church. Indeed, they feel compelled to do so in light of the invigorating teachings of the council.

Karl Rahner sees the entire church as the sacrament of the world's salvation. It is the organized society that continues to proclaim God's self-communication in the person of Christ to all of humankind (or as much of humanity as it can reach). The church is the result of God's grace, and it stands as the primary sacrament of God's loving and saving presence in the world. The local church, the parish, base community or other congregation of worship *is* that church present and active in a particular place.

Rahner is careful to note, however, that the local churches do not enjoy the same indefectibility in holiness and truth that has been assured to the church universal. That is to say, local churches are neither infallible nor sinless!

The local church is visible, a social entity, a particular portion of God's people, a group of individuals from a particular culture, class and ethnic background. They are sinners and they are virtuous. Many belong, but are lukewarm. Many only partially identify with the church or find themselves in some tension with it. Still, this concrete community, with all its human characters and failings, strives to manifest God's mercy and grace to those around it. It steadfastly points to God's powerful presence in the world.

In the parish the church exists in the concrete, in everyday life; it celebrates the death of the Lord, breaks the bread of the word of God, prays, loves and bears the cross of human existence. "The highest truth which can be applied to the church as a whole," Rahner said, "is in fact asserted of the local community itself, namely that in it Christ himself, his gospel, his love and the unity of believers are present." The local parish community, far from being a mere minor administrative unit of a large religious organization called the church, is actually the concrete reality of the church. It is the presence of Christ, in the word, in the eucharistic meal, and in the love, that unites those who share in them.

Holy Spirit

After the council, Yves Congar wrote of the local church in the context of his studies on the Holy Spirit. The Spirit of God is not only present in the local church, it makes the church, animates it, gives it life and builds it up. God's Holy Spirit is the principle of the communion of the church, that mystical communion that joins the members and joins the churches together with one another, and with Christ their Lord. The Spirit is given to the community and to the individuals who are baptized into it.

The Spirit founds the solidarity that we call "the communion of the saints" and that consists in living and behaving as conscious members of an organic whole. This Spirit-sponsored communion calls for concrete, human and personal relationships, like those between family members, relationships of closeness and mutual dependence. Congar said that the visible expression of Christian solidarity is the charity that the Holy Spirit places in our hearts, both sublime and very concrete and practical. It finds expression in simple and direct ways—a greeting, a handshake, an embrace, an act of kindness.

The church is generated where there is faith, a faith that is handed on. This communication of faith, both giving and receiving it, is an interpersonal process. One person shares faith with another. Individual Christian women and men prepare others to receive faith, baptize and confirm them in the faith, form and guide them as they mature in faith and love. This all takes place in a local community called church.

The church comes into existence in a special way and expresses itself most perfectly in the celebration of the Lord's Supper. It is an ancient axiom that "the church makes the eucharist, and the eucharist makes the church." The eucharistic assembly is the primary manifestation of the church. It is the event in which the local church best expresses itself. But it is also a profoundly catholic event—the local community gathered around the table of the Lord is supremely conscious of and connected to the church worldwide, as well as to Christ himself. This awareness is spoken explicitly in the canon of the mass: "Lord, remember your church throughout the world."

Another manifestation of this sense of communion, this linkage to the larger church, is through the pastor. The parish priest, or another person appointed in his stead, is assigned to the role by the local bishop. This initial authorization and the subsequent ministry exercised by the pastor under the authority of the bishop constitutes an additional connection with the wider church, a connection integral to the catholicity of the local church.

Joseph Komonchak, a prominent American ecclesiologist, emphasizes the irreplaceable human element in the church's existence. The constitutive principles of the church (at any level) include: the call of God, the word of Christ, the presence of the Spirit, the celebration of the eucharist, the fellowship of love and the apostolic ministry (i.e., leadership in connection with that of the apostles). Where these principles generate a community, it *is* the church, not merely a part of the church, but the full reality of the people of God and the dwelling place of the Spirit.

In terms of spiritual reality nothing more is realized on any wider or higher level of the church's life than is realized in an authentic local church. But this local realization obviously includes human persons. The constitutive principles must be believed and accepted by the free actions of individuals. The acts of faith, hope and love are human acts. Men and women, under the power of the Spirit, are moved to take those actions, and, in doing so, they build up the church. The local congregation, a group of unique individuals, a human community existing in a particular place and time, *is* the realization of the church. So the human community in a specific place is also one of the constitutive principles of the church.

The human-ness of the local church also implies its inculturation. The human community is part and parcel of its surrounding culture, its context, its geography, its history, its environment. These elements are not simply the stage setting for the life of the local church, they are part of its essence, part of its very nature as church.

The local inculturation of the church has obvious implications for its mission and activities. The parish must act where it is. It must "do its thing" in its own cultural and historical place. The local community is called upon to assess its role in its own surrounding, in its own time. It must discern what witness and action it needs to take in its own neighborhood, with its own resources. The mission of the local church grows, at least in part, out of its sense of locality.

These local churches are, and are conscious of being, in communion with one another. They are oriented outward as well as inward. They are tenaciously tied to the diocesan communion, the national communion and the universal communion of churches. Indeed, the communion among them *is* the universal church, the one, holy, catholic and apostolic church. The church universal exists *in* and *out of* local churches.

One manifestation of communion, one living linkage to the larger church, is the leadership of the local community, usually the priest-pastor, but sometimes a sister or a deacon or a layperson. That pastoral leader is assigned or appointed or accepted by the diocesan bishop, and ministers subject to his authority. This is both a source of authentication and a connection with the church's hierarchy.

The relationship of the local churches to the diocesan and universal churches is *not* like that of members to their federation (individual states to the United States) or like the parts to a whole (individual pieces to a jigsaw puzzle). Rather they are mutually inclusive. The local churches and the diocesan and universal churches exist within one another. They live in communion. Every local church is a realization of the diocese and of the one church of Christ, and the diocesan church and the one Catholic Church exist in and out of the local churches.

This mutual inclusion demands attitudes and actions in concert, a real communion of minds, hearts and activity, like that for which Christ prayed at the Last Supper, "that they may be one" (Jn 17:11).

Sources and Readings

Abbott, W., ed. *The Documents of Vatican II*. New York: America Press, 1966.

Congar, Y. *I Believe in the Holy Spirit*. 2 vols. New York: Seabury, 1983.

Flannery, A., ed. *Vatican Council II: The Conciliar and Post Conciliar Documents*. Rev. ed. Boston: St. Paul Editions, 1988.

Floristan, C. *The Parish—Eucharistic Community*. Notre Dame, Ind.: Fides, 1964.

Kilian, S. *Theological Models of the Parish*. New York: Alba House, 1976.

Komonchak, J. "The Church Universal as the Communion of Local Churches." In *Where Does the Church Stand?* Edited by G. Alberigo and G. Gutiérrez. Vol. 146 in *Concilium*. New York: Seabury, 1981.

——————— ."The Local Realization of the Church." In *The Reception of Vatican II*. Edited by G. Alberigo, J.-P. Jossua and J. Komonchak. Washington D.C.: Catholic University of America Press, 1987.

Lennan, R. *The Ecclesiology of Karl Rahner*. Oxford: Clarendon Press, 1995.

The Local Church and Catholicity, an issue of *The Jurist* 52, 1 (1992):1–586; cf. especially J. Komonchak, "The Local Church and the Church Catholic: The Contemporary Theological Problematic," 416–47.

McBrien, R. "The Parish We Are Shaping." In *Parish: A Place for Worship*. Edited by M. Searle. Collegeville, Minn.: Liturgical Press, 1980, pp. 13–28.

Murnion, P. "Parish: Covenant Community." *Church* 12, 1 (Spring 1996): 5–10.

Tillard, J. *Church of Churches: The Ecclesiology of Communion*. Collegeville, Minn.: Liturgical Press, 1992.

4

The Parish and the Church's Social Teaching

There are several principles enshrined in the church's rich heritage of social teachings which undergird the innate dignity and legitimate autonomy of local churches. These principles of social philosophy confirm the identity and stature of stable human communities, including parishes and other local Catholic communities. The church considers these principles to be part of the natural law, God's law written in the human heart. The church has acknowledged that the principles apply within the church itself as well as in society at large. The principles to be briefly examined here are: (1) the freedom or right of association, (2) the notion of the common good and the principles of (3) solidarity and (4) subsidiarity.

The Right of Association

Humans are social beings. There is a natural propensity for human persons to live in societies, and this basic natural impulse grounds the right of association. To join or to create societies or associations is a fundamental human right, long and widely recognized. As long as these associations are not evil, unjust or dangerous, they are not to be prohibited or unreasonably regulated (*RN* 49ff.)

It follows from this natural human right of association that the associations that people found and join do themselves have rights. That is, the existence of the associations and the exercise of their legitimate activities must be respected by the larger societies within which they live.

The Second Vatican Council recognized the natural human right to associate for religious purposes and explicitly encouraged the exercise of this right of association within the church (*DH* 4, *AA* 19 and 24). The church's Code of Canon Law, enacted in 1983, acknowledges and declares this basic right of all the faithful:

> The Christian faithful are at liberty freely to found and to govern associations for charitable and religious purposes or for the promotion of the Christian vocation in the world; they are free to hold meetings to pursue these purposes in common. (C. 215; see also cc. 298–299)

The associations referred to in these documents are usually thought of as those organizations, groups or societies established within local churches which parishioners join and whose meetings they attend. However, the principle of association applies as well to the local congregations themselves. The faithful people have the right to join or even to found local churches. In the eighteenth and nineteenth centuries in the United States the people, groups of immigrant Catholics, frequently started their own parishes. They did not do so against the wishes of the church's hierarchy; it was (and is) for the bishop to establish the congregation canonically as a parish and to assign it a pastor. But the people often took the initiative, organized the community and then asked for the bishop's approval.

The point is that, even prior to the official establishment of a parish and after it has been long in existence, the natural right of the people to join, actively participate in and sustain their religious community endures. The local congregation remains in communion with and subject to the authority of the larger church, but it also remains as a legitimate expression of the right of the Christian faithful to associate for religious purposes. This gives local churches a dignity, stature and permanence that must be respected.

The Common Good

The common good demands that we raise our attention from our own needs and desires and look to what is in the interests of all. It calls for a constant consideration of what is best for the community as well as for the individuals who belong to the community.

The concept of the common good is a central feature of modern Catholic social teaching. It was developed over the years, notably in the encyclical letters of Pope John XXIII *On Christianity and Social Progress* (*Mater et Magistra,* 1961) and *Peace on Earth* (*Pacem in Terris,* 1963). It was formally described at the Second Vatican Council in this way:

> The common good of society consists in the sum total of the conditions of social life under which human persons are able to pursue their own perfection fully and expeditiously; most of all it consists in the observance of the rights and duties of the human person. (*DH* 6)

The common good is not in opposition to personal or communal rights, but it actually consists in the observance of the rights and duties of persons and communities.

The common good requires the establishment of those conditions that are necessary for persons to enter into the community and to participate fully in its life.

The common good is a principle of *inclusion* insofar as it insists that the needs and interests of all members of the community be considered, especially those of the less advantaged or marginalized members.

The common good is a principle of *equality* in that it calls for equal treatment of all members of the community, to the greatest extent possible. Special privileges and favored status create inequalities that tend to undermine the common good.

The common good is a principle of *participation* that is, it requires that all are to have access to the benefits of belonging to the community, to the protection of their rights, to open discussion and consensus in pursuit of specific goals.

Finally, the common good is a principle of *coordination.* It demands that all the members of the community and all of the subgroups within it take the common good into consideration, balance their claims over against it, make their decisions in light of it and bring their interests into line with it.

The church's own rules call for individuals and groups within it to attend to the common good in the exercise of their rights (c. 233.1).

The common good of each local church, which is the goal toward which its members and groups must strive, can be described in terms of the ability of its members: *common good of local church*

—to grow into mature disciples of Christ,
—to hear and respond to the word of God,
—to offer praise to God and to celebrate the sacraments,
—to give common witness to their faith, hope and love,
—to rejoice in the communion of the entire people of God.

The Principle of Solidarity

Solidarity describes a commitment on the part of those who form a community to participate in the life of that community in a way that promotes the common good.

Pope John Paul II developed the notion of solidarity in his encyclical letter *On Social Concerns* (1987):

> It is above all a question of interdependence, sensed as a system determining relationship in the contemporary world, in its economic, cultural, political and religious elements, and accepted as a moral category. When interdependence becomes recognized in this way, the correlative response as a moral and social attitude, as a "virtue," is solidarity....it is a firm and persevering determination to commit oneself to the common good. (*SRS* 38) *human interdependance*

This sense of mutual responsibility and care, based on the recognition of human interdependence, has application locally as well as nationally and globally. It has a place in communities of the faithful as well as in the community of nations.

The exercise of solidarity within each society is valid when its members recognize one another as persons....Solidarity helps us to see the "other"—whether a person, people or nation—not just as some kind of instrument..., but as our "neighbor," a "helper" (see Gn 2:18–20), to be made a sharer on a par with ourselves in the banquet of life to which all are equally invited by God. (*SRS* 39)

Solidarity not only has a place in the local church, it is the glue that holds congregations together. It is part of their texture, their very warp and woof. Solidarity helps to define Catholic parishes as human and religious communities whose members' lives are intertwined in many ways. Solidarity obliges attention to the needs of the weak and disadvantaged within the local community, as well as of those further away. Solidarity lends strength and stability to the community and gives impetus to its actions on behalf of justice and charity.

The Principle of Subsidiarity

Most important of all the church's social teachings for the identity of the local church is the principle of subsidiarity. It means that local communities, those made up of individual human persons, like parishes, must be respected and allowed a maximum of self-determination.

The principle was most recently restated officially by Pope John Paul II in his encyclical letter *One Hundredth Year* (after the 1891 encyclical *Rerum Novarum, Centesimus Annus*, 1991):

> Here again the principle of subsidiarity must be respected: A community of a higher order should not interfere in the internal life of a community of a lower order, depriving the latter of its functions, but rather should support it in case of need and help to coordinate its activity with the activities of the rest of society, always with a view to the common good. (*CA* 48)

Fifty years earlier, in his major encyclical on the reconstruction of the social order, Pope Pius XI spoke of subsidiarity as "that most weighty principle, which cannot be set aside or changed, [and which] remains fixed and unshaken in social philosophy":

> Just as it is gravely wrong to take from individuals what they can accomplish by their own initiative and industry and give it to the community, so also it is an injustice and at the same time a grave

evil and disturbance of right order to assign a greater and higher association what lesser and subordinate organizations can do. For every social activity ought of its very nature to furnish help to the members of the body social, and never destroy and absorb them. (*QA* 79)

Pope John XXIII repeated this definition in his letter *Mater et Magistra,* and he called it the "guiding principle of subsidiary function" (*MM* 53).

The principle of subsidiarity is obviously firmly imbedded in Catholic social teaching. Its application within the church itself is also well grounded. This was explicitly affirmed by Pope Pius XII in 1946 (Feb. 20) and by Pope Paul VI in 1969 (Oct. 27).

The principle of subsidiarity was one of the guiding principles adopted by those engaged in the revision of the Code of Canon Law after the Vatican Council. It was formally approved as a guiding principle by the Episcopal Synod of 1967: "Careful attention is to be given to the greater application of the principle of subsidiarity within the Church" (Preface to the Code).

Since the church is a visible, organized, complex, human community, the principle of subsidiary function must find full application within it, as well as outside it in secular societies.

What does this mean for parishes and similar local communities in relationship to their dioceses? The principle of subsidiarity affirms their right to exist, to make their own decisions and to take actions in keeping with their mission and goals. They are always to be in communion with the other local churches in the diocese and with the diocesan bishop, but they are not to be smothered or subsumed by the diocesan organization. They must have room to live.

Subsidiarity implies that local communities exercise appropriate initiatives and self-direction. It does not imply complete autonomy or aloof independence; local churches are in communion with one another. But dioceses exist to support, assist and coordinate the activities of parishes and other communities, not to dominate them or displace their rightful activities. The principle of subsidiarity requires that local communities of the faithful be allowed and encouraged to pursue a maximum range of ecclesial action.

Sources and Readings

Christiansen, D. "The Common Good and the Politics of Self-Interest." In *Beyond Individualism: Toward a Retrieval of Moral Discourse in America.* Edited by D. Gelpi. Notre Dame, Ind.: University of Notre Dame Press, 1989, pp. 54–86.

Hollenbach, D. "The Common Good Revisited." *Theological Studies* 50 (1989): 70–94.

—————. *Justice, Peace, and Human Rights: American Catholic Social Ethics in a Pluralistic World.* New York: Crossroad, 1988.

Proclaiming Justice and Peace: Papal Documents from "Rerum Novarum" through "Centesimus Annus." Edited by M. Walsh and B. Davies. Mystic, Conn.: Twenty-Third Publications, 1991.

5

The Parish in Canon Law

Canon law is the name for the official rules of the Roman Catholic Church. The central and coordinating body of canons (rules) for the Western (i.e., Latin Rite) church is the Code of Canon Law, most recently revised in 1983. The section of the Code on "Parishes, Pastors and Parochial Vicars" (cc. 515–552) contains much that is new, as a result of the actions of the Second Vatican Council. The identity of the parish in these revised canons is clearer and more accurate than ever before.

The focus in this chapter is on the parish *community* as such rather than on the pastor or the pastoral ministry within the community.

A Community of the Faithful

parish *

In earlier canon law the parish was understood to be an institution to serve the spiritual needs of the faithful. At the same time it was described as a "benefice" (i.e., an office with a source of income attached to it), primarily for the assignment of revenue to the pastor. The elements of the notion of a parish were: a territorial section of the diocese, a church building, an assigned Catholic population and a pastor who was responsible for the care of souls *(cura animarum)*.

Now, in the revised Code, a parish is defined as a community of Christian people. Canon 515.1 states:

> A parish is a definite community of the Christian faithful estab-
> lished on a stable basis within a particular church; the pastoral care
> of the parish is entrusted to a pastor as its own shepherd under the
> authority of the diocesan bishop.

The term community was deliberately chosen to signify something more than a "territory," more than a "portion of the People
of God" (which is the way a diocese is defined, c. 369) and more
than a mere group or gathering of people. *Community* means a
group of individuals and families who know each other, share
common values and relate with one another. They live near each
other in a neighborhood or part of town. Or, in the case of personal, nonterritorial parishes, they are united by language, ethnic
origin or some other common interest.

The members of the community interact with one another and
realize that they are dependent upon one another in their religious lives. They worship together, grow in the faith together and
face the crises of life together. They join in celebrating family
births and baptisms, marriages and funerals. There are multiple
bonds between them.

The term *definite* in the definition simply means defined. The
community is clearly designated in some way, for example, as the
people living in a determined area of the city or county, or the
Spanish-speaking, or those of Vietnamese origin or the students,
faculty and staff of a college or university.

> As a general rule a parish is to be territorial, that is, it embraces all
> the Christian faithful within a certain territory; whenever it is
> judged useful, however, personal parishes are to be established
> based upon rite, language, the nationality of the Christian faithful
> within some territory or even upon some other determining fac-
> tor. (C. 518)

The words "established on a stable basis" in the definition
imply that the community is not transient but permanent. A
parish is not a one-time gathering, a month-long assembly or a
three-month summer camp. It enjoys stability. The community
members foresee being together for the long haul, even though
many individuals may leave and be replaced by others over
time.

"Within a particular church" simply means that every parish is established within a diocese. "Each and every diocese...is to be divided into distinct parts or parishes" (c. 374). Parishes make up the communion of local churches that is called a diocese.

The "pastoral care" of the community is entrusted to a parish priest as the community's own pastor. The normal arrangement is for each parish to have a priest-pastor. However, the canons provide for other options. Several neighboring parishes can be entrusted to the same pastor (c. 526.1). One or several parishes can be entrusted to a team of priests, or, when there is a lack of priests, the pastoral care of a parish can be exercised by a deacon or other person who is not a priest (i.e., a religious sister or brother, or a lay man or woman), or even by a community of such persons (c. 517.2). In these latter cases, that is, when the pastoral care is given to nonpriests, a priest-pastor is appointed to supervise the pastoral care. He may reside in a neighboring parish or at a greater distance.

Whoever exercises that pastoral care does so "under the authority of the diocesan bishop." This is part of the bishop's supervisory role, and it is also one of the bonds that link local churches together in the diocesan communion. The bishop appoints the pastor or other pastoral care-giver(s), and, when circumstances require it, can remove them (cc. 523, 1740).

Those Who Belong to the Parish Community

All of the baptized Catholics within the territory of the parish who remain in communion with the church are eligible to be members of the parish (cc. 96, 102, 204). Or, if the parish is non-territorial, that is, established for a community of people based on their ethnic background or language or affiliation (e.g., with a university or military base), then all of the Catholic members of that group qualify for membership.

> Those baptized are fully in communion with the Catholic Church on this earth who are joined with Christ in its visible structure by the bonds of profession of faith, of the sacraments and of ecclesiastical governance. (C. 205; see *LG* 14)

In actual practice, parish membership is often a matter of personal preference or family choice. While canon law still assigns Catholics to their "proper pastor" on the basis of their residence (c. 107.1), it also allows them to participate in the eucharist or go to confession anywhere (cc. 1248.1, 991). The concept of community assumes major importance. That is, when people join a parish community, participate regularly and support the activities of that community with their energy and contributions, they create a sense of belonging (c. 1262).

When it comes to the milestone events in a family's religious life, namely, baptisms, first communions, confirmations, marriages and funerals, canon law clearly prefers the parish church, but never so strictly that these events cannot take place elsewhere (cc. 857.2, 914, 890, 1115, 1177). Again, in normal circumstances the community of belonging is the proper place for these events.

Pastors' responsibilities are assigned in terms of the parish community entrusted to them. They are to exercise pastoral care in that community (c. 519), see that the word of God is announced to those living therein (c. 528.1), make the eucharist the center of the parish congregation (c. 528.2), strive to know the faithful and visit the families of the parish (c. 529.1) and promote the parish communion and its sense of communion with the diocese and universal church (c. 529.2).

Ultimately, for baptized and believing adult Catholics, belonging comes down to personal intentions and actions, that is, the internal disposition of solidarity with the parish community and the external expressions of participation in its life.

The practice of crossing parish boundaries to belong to another parish community is now recognized as legitimate. Some dioceses have explicitly affirmed this possibility.

There are some categories of persons whose affiliation with the parish community is less clear. Catechumens, that is, those who have asked to be incorporated into the church and are preparing for baptism, are already cherished participants in the life of the parish (c. 206). Those Catholics living in irregular marriages (i.e., unions not canonically recognized) are still very much part of the parish community (see FC 79–84). Baptized Christians who belong to another church or to no church at all but may be related to Catholic parish members or prefer to attend a local Catholic church may be welcomed. They should not be admitted to full sacramental communion until they seek it and are suitably prepared for it, but they are similar to "precatechumens." Likewise, those baptized Catholics who are transients or who live within the parish but never attend church services should be welcomed and cared for, but their sense of belonging to the parish community is tenuous.

Active Involvement

Canon law does not envision parishioners as passive recipients of pastoral care. Members of the parish are seen as and encouraged to be fully active and engaged participants in the life and activities of their parish community. Various forms of this participation are detailed below under "activities of the parish." However, there are two new instruments for active involvement that deserve special attention here: (1) the parish pastoral council and (2) the parish finance council.

The pastoral council is a child of the Second Vatican Council (see *LG* Chapter IV and *AA* 26). It reflects a changed attitude toward the laity, one which views laypersons as empowered and responsible within the church as well as in the world. The parish pastoral council is one vehicle for the expression of lay voice and wisdom. It is one way for parishioners to participate in making the policies and decisions that guide the parish community.

Canon law describes the pastoral council as a means for the Christian faithful and those who share in pastoral care of the parish to "help in fostering pastoral activity" (c. 536.1). The pastor, or the person in charge of the parish, heads the council, and it is consultative to that pastoral leader (c. 536.2). However, the pastoral council should be a collaborative group that works with the pastor and others exercising ministry in the parish. The scope of its activity can be very broad, but its central task may be planning for the future of the community rather than involving itself in the day-to-day oversight of the parish. Many dioceses provide valuable guidelines and formation programs for parish pastoral councils.

The bishops who took part in the 1987 Synod on the Laity spoke to lay participation in their parishes and parish councils:

> It is in the parish that most Catholics learn that they have been constituted as church (or a portion of the church) and that, at the same time, they experience how to form the church. The collaboration of clergy and laity is needed to achieve this. This collaboration requires the consultation of the laity to determine the pastoral needs and aspirations of the community. A more fitting way to reach this goal is the establishment of a pastoral council in which all can take part. (Synod Propositions, 9, *Origins* 17, 29 [1987]: 502)

The bishops went on to speak about the right and responsibility of laypersons to participate actively in the life and formation of the church. The bishops explained that laypersons exercise this right in a special way by "listening to one another and establishing dialogue" in discernment toward consensus in councils.

The parish finance council, usually smaller than the pastoral council and with a narrower range of responsibility, is another new instrument for lay participation in the life of the parish. It consists of members of the Christian faithful who are to aid the pastor in the administration of parish goods (cc. 537, 1280). The administration of parish finances and properties can be burdensome; the duties of an administrator of church property are summarized in canons 1282 to 1287 of the Code. Good administration is of vital importance to the life and health of the parish community. There is also an obligation to report regularly to the rest of the parish community on the financial situation of the parish (c. 1287.2).

The Parish as Juridic Person: Subject of Rights and Duties

Parishes are canonically established by the diocesan bishop. They may and often do exist as communities before the bishop takes this action, but his letter or decree formally constitutes the community as a parish. Only the diocesan bishop is empowered to take the action of setting up, suppressing or notably altering a parish. He may not take such actions before he hears the presbyteral council (priests' senate) on the matter (c. 515.2). The canonical establishment or alteration of a parish is viewed as a very serious matter, one that impacts the diocesan communion of churches. Hence, only the head of the diocese and chief minister of its governance, the bishop, can take such an action, and he can do so only after consulting his primary collaborators and advisors, the presbyterate.

Parishes are "juridic persons" from the moment of their establishment (c. 515.3). This means that they have legal "personality"; they are recognized canonically and have standing in the church's canonical system, just as corporations or business partnerships have in state legal systems.

Juridic persons are the subjects of rights and obligations in the church, just as individuals are (c. 113.2). (The specific rights and obligations of parishes are listed below in Chapter 6.) Juridic persons can own property, take legal actions and vindicate their rights. The community of the Christian faithful along with its pastor constitutes the parish juridic person.

Juridic persons are permanent, perpetual of their very nature, that is, they do not expire as legal entities with the passage of time *juridic* (c. 120). This permanent status illustrates the canonical dignity and autonomy of the parish, and it underlines the gravity of the merger or suppression of parishes, by which one or more juridic persons can be extinguished.

A parish is considered to be a public, noncollegial juridic person, an aggregate of persons (c. 115). Its "public" nature means that it is set up by a competent church authority and that it fulfills a function in keeping with the common good of the church (c. 116). It is considered "noncollegial" because its juridic actions are ultimately determined not by the members of the community but by the pastor, who represents it juridically and acts in its name (cc. 532, 118). This does not mean that the pastor alone deliberates and decides for the parish, but rather that he must concur with the final decision for it to be canonically effective. In other words, neither the nature of the parish as juridic person nor the pastor's role as its representative stand in the way of thoroughgoing collegial activity and decision making.

The parish owns the property and goods that it acquires by

purchase or donation or any other means (cc. 1255, 1256). The property is considered to be "ecclesiastical goods," regulated by canon law (c. 1257). The pastor, or someone appointed in his place, is the administrator of the parish property (c. 1279). He or she is responsible for the administration of all the property and assets that belong to the parish, even though the pastor is assisted by a parish finance council and other personnel on staff (cc. 1281–1288, 537).

Activities of the Parish Community in Canon Law

The Code of Canon Law specifies or implies many activities that are obligatory or at least appropriate for parishes. The following are clusters of those functions or activities indicated in the canons which ought to take place in parishes and other local congregations. The functions are often stated in terms of the pastor's duties, but they involve and affect the entire parish community and, in a very real way, are the responsibilities of the whole community. The list is not exhaustive.

1. Proclamation of the word of God, preaching, teaching, catechesis, formation in faith, Catholic education of adults and children:

cc. 211, 213, 217—basic rights and duties,
   c. 528.1—the pastor's role,
cc. 757, 759, 761—ministry of the word,
cc. 762, 767–771—preaching,
cc. 773–774, 776–777, 779—catechetical instruction,
cc. 788–789—the catechumenate,
cc. 793–794, 796, 798—Catholic education.

2. Worship of God, sacramental celebrations, prayer, works of penance and charity, sacramentals, liturgy of the hours, funeral rites, sacramental records:

cc. 210, 213–214—basic rights and duties,
cc. 528.2, 530, 534, 535—the pastor's role,
cc. 834, 835.4, 836–837, 839—the sacred liturgy,
cc. 840, 843—sacraments,
cc. 851, 857–858, 861, 877—baptism,
cc. 890, 895—confirmation,

cc. 897–899, 912, 914, 920–922, 934, 937, 941–942—holy eucharist,

cc. 959, 986–989—penance,

cc. 998, 1001–1002—anointing of the sick,

cc. 1063, 1115, 1121, 1128—marriage,

cc. 1173–1174—liturgy of the hours,

cc. 1176–1177, 1182—funerals,

cc. 1245, 1246–1253—feast days and penitential days.

3. Gathering, caring for, ordering and building the parish community, communicating with the community members, visiting families, helping the sick and the poor, promoting family life:

cc. 212, 216, 226—basic rights and duties,

cc. 519, 529—the pastor's role,

c. 536—parish pastoral council,

c. 545—parochial vicar,

c. 1285—support works of charity.

4. Acquiring and maintaining suitable facilities, for example, church building, rectory, cemetery, and administering resources, accounts, contracts and payments, for example, collections, savings, fund drives:

cc. 222, 231.2—basic rights and duties,

cc. 532, 533—pastor's role,

c. 537—parish finance council,

cc. 1214–1221—church,

cc. 1240–1243—cemetery,

cc. 1254–1269, 1279–1310—temporal goods, administration.

5. Mission outreach and support, spreading the gospel message, evangelizing, promoting vocations:

cc. 211, 225.1, 233.1—basic rights and duties,

c. 528.1—the pastor's role,

c. 771.2—evangelization,

cc. 781, 786, 788, 789, 791—missionary action.

6. Promoting social justice, witness and actions on behalf of the human community:

cc. 215, 222.2, 225.2—basic rights and duties,

c. 768.2—preaching social justice.

These are only those actions and functions of the local church that have been enshrined in the canons. They reflect the long history of the Catholic parish tradition, but they in no way limit the initiatives and additional activities of present-day parishes.

One of the above-mentioned canons is an especially good illustration of the parish community's responsibility for a ministry:

> Pastors of souls are obliged to see to it that their own ecclesial community furnishes the Christian faithful assistance so that the matrimonial state is maintained in a Christian spirit and makes progress toward perfection. (C. 1063)

The canon goes on to spell out the various forms that the marriage ministry should include, for example, ongoing instruction, personal preparation for marriage, appropriate liturgical celebration and support systems after marriage.

Other Catholic Communities

Canon law recognizes that there are many local congregations of Catholics that do not have the status of parishes. Some are called "quasi-parishes," parish-like communities that simply have not yet been erected as parishes (c. 516.1). For example, a community may lack the financial resources to assure its continuance, or the transiency of an immigrant group might make its stability problematic.

In addition, the canons recognize other kinds of local communities for which the bishop is obliged to provide pastoral care (c. 516.2). Mission churches, campus congregations, chaplaincies of various kinds (e.g., for hospitals, military bases, prisons, religious houses, migrant camps), pastoral centers, shrine churches or oratories (with rectors rather than pastors) are examples of parish-like communities that frequently do not have the canonical status of parishes (cc. 556ff., 564ff., 1223ff., 1230ff.).

"Intentional eucharistic communities," that is, Catholic groups that come together on a voluntary but stable basis for purposes of worship and witness, also exist and are sometimes acknowledged by the diocesan church.

All of these nonparochial communities are analogous to parishes, that is, they are similar to parishes in some ways and differ from them in others. However, they are more like parishes than they are unlike them. They are obliged to assume the responsibilities of communion with the diocese and the church universal, and they should be accorded the rights, respect and services that befit their dignity as legitimate local congregations of the faithful. They are real churches in the New Testament and theological meaning of the word. Christ is truly present in them (*LG* 26).

"Small church communities," renewal groups and bible discussion and prayer groups are welcome contemporary developments *within* parishes. These subgroups, somewhat like the house churches of the first centuries, are healthy manifestations of church life and provide a precious context for worship, faith sharing, religious growth and prophetic witness. Some groups display remarkable vitality and stability and provide an ecclesial experience on a human, interpersonal scale. They must remain connected to the larger church, parish or diocese, in close communion, and resist any tendencies toward divisiveness or isolation. Small church communities are a sign of hope and a work of God's grace.

Sources and Readings

The Canon Law: Letter and Spirit. Canon Law Society of Great Britain and Ireland. Collegeville, Minn.: Liturgical Press, 1996.

The Code of Canon Law (Latin-English Edition). Washington, D.C.: CLSA, 1983.

Code of Canon Law Annotated. Edited by E. Caparros, M. Theriault and J. Thorn. Montreal: Wilson & Lafleur Ltd., 1993.

The Code of Canon Law: A Text and Commentary. Edited by J. Coriden, T. Green and D. Heinstchel. New York: Paulist Press, London: Geoffrey Chapman, 1985.

The Code of Canons of the Eastern Churches (Latin-English Edition). Washington, D.C.: CLSA, 1992.

Deegan, A., ed. *Developing a Vibrant Parish Pastoral Council.* Clearwater, Fla.: Conference for Pastoral Planning, 1994.

Huels, J. *The Catechumenate and the Law.* Chicago: Liturgy Training Publications, 1994.

John Paul II. Apostolic Exhortation *On The Family* (*Familiaris Consortio*, December 15, 1981). Washington, D.C.: USCC, 1982.

NCCB Hispanic Affairs Committee. "Communion and Mission: A Guide for Bishops and Pastoral Leaders on Small Church Communities." *Origins* 25, 31 (January 25, 1996): 513–22.

Provost, J. "Parish Membership—Who Gets Counted?" *The Priest*, July–August 1980, 30–38.

Sacred Congregation for Bishops. *Directory on the Pastoral Office of Bishops*. Ottawa: Canadian Catholic Conference, 1974.

6
Parish Rights and Obligations

One of the distinctive features of the 1983 revision of the Code of Canon Law was an enumeration of the rights and obligations of individual members of the Christian faithful (cc. 208–223). This unprecedented articulation of the rights and duties of Catholic Church members was repeated in the 1991 Code of Canons for the Eastern Churches (cc. 10–26). However, a similar list of the rights and obligations of *local communities* of the faithful was notably absent from both of these modern codes, even though it had been specifically requested by prominent writers during the time of their revision.

By their very establishment, parishes are juridic persons in canon law, that is, they are the subjects of rights and obligations (cc. 515.3, 113.2). The foundations for such rights and obligations are firmly grounded on the biblical, theological, historical and social teachings that have been explored in the foregoing chapters of this book. But the rights and duties of the communities have not yet been officially addressed. Their number and extent still await clear description. It is a piece of unfinished business that remained after the canon law revisions following the Second Vatican Council were completed.

Many rights and duties of parishes are implied, rather than stated, in the canons. Others are derived from the very nature of the local churches themselves, that is, from their very essence as "definite communities of the Christian faithful established on a stable basis within a particular church" (c. 515.1). What follows is an attempt to articulate a list of those canonical rights and obligations.

Before getting into the actual list of community rights and duties, it is important to realize why they are necessary. The reasons are found in: (1) the theology of the local church and (2) the church's social teaching about subsidiarity.

1. The church in its most authentic reality is a communion of churches. It is built up from below by local congregations that are in communion with one another. At every level the church is a communion of communities. The dignity and legitimate autonomy of local churches must be affirmed, especially in these times, of strong centralizing tendencies, and the assertion of their rights and obligations is one important way of doing that.

2. The principle of subsidiary function insists that the internal life of local communities must be respected and not usurped or dominated from outside. This applies to parishes and other local congregations, and one way of demonstrating that is by focusing on their rights and duties.

A List of Parish Rights and Obligations

1. Existence

A parish right more fundamental than all others is the right to come into existence, to have that existence acknowledged and to continue in existence. Dioceses are required to be divided into parishes (c. 374.1). Parishes and other local communities are not optional. They are legitimate and necessary manifestations of church life.

Once a community of faith has been formed and recognized, it should be allowed to remain, to live, to act and to grow. Canon law gives a strong presumption in favor of its endurance in being. Once a community is erected as a parish, it has juridic personality (c. 515.3), and a juridic person is of its nature perpetual. It continues in being unless and until it is legitimately suppressed or has ceased all activity for a hundred years (c. 120.1).

That is the way that the canonical tradition expresses the continuity and permanence of parishes. The natural right of association as well as the principles of solidarity and subsidiarity also argues for the stability of local churches. In addition, as the Second Vatican Council taught, these local congregations are like the churches of the New Testament. The church universal, and Christ himself, is truly present in them (*LG* 26). They are not ephemeral or transitory gatherings but enduring communities.

Parishes should not be suppressed or merged with others unless they are evidently no longer viable. The impossibility of their continued life must be clearly demonstrated. A shortage of priests for pastoral leadership is not an adequate reason to suppress or combine parishes. Canon law strongly recommends liturgies of the word and group prayer in the absence of sacred ministers (c. 1248.2), clearly implying that the life and worship of the community must continue even when priestly leadership is absent.

The presbyteral council must be heard in advance of any action to suppress or merge parishes (c. 515.2), and those with rights or interests in the parish should also be consulted (cc. 50, 1222.2).

2. Maintain Communion

Communion with other Catholic churches is a unique privilege and responsibility of every parish. The observable signs of this spiritual union are the profession of our common faith, the celebration of the sacraments, and recognition of the church's governance (c. 206). These are in addition to the invisible bonds of communion: God's grace, Christ's presence and the Spirit's power.

Each local community has the right and obligation to maintain active communion with the church; it is to fulfill diligently its duties toward the universal church and the diocese (c. 209). Each parish is to observe obediently the teachings and policies of the diocesan bishop (c. 212.1) and to observe the church's discipline (i.e., canon law, c. 392.1). The bishop's pastoral visitation of the parish is a sign of this right and duty of communion (c. 396).

Parishes should contribute to and receive assistance from the other local churches with which they are in communion. They are to assist with the worship needs, apostolic efforts, works of charity and sustenance of ministers in other communities as well as in their own, depending on their means and resources (cc. 209.2, 529.2, 1261–1263). This mutual material and spiritual support is often mediated through the diocese.

3. Equality

Each local congregation of the faithful shares in the "true equality in dignity and action whereby all cooperate in the building up of the Body of Christ" (c. 208). In other words, among Catholic communities there is a fundamental equality that transcends their differences. Parishes differ in number of members, size of territory, age of establishment, quality of buildings, location, economic wealth, ethnic composition and in other ways. But they are radically equal as congregations of the faithful. They may not be treated as privileged or second-rate, some favored with careful attention, others relatively neglected.

Catholic parishes are equal "in virtue of their rebirth in Christ" (c. 208), and each has the right to be accorded the dignity and respect due to members of the diocesan family of faith communities. Each has a right to its good name and reputation (c. 220).

This claim of equality among local congregations does not ignore canonical distinctions between parishes and nonparishes, shrines and mission churches, chaplaincies and intentional communities. Underlying these canonical differences is a fundamental and equal stature as authentic churches, stable gatherings of Christians in which the Spirit abides.

4. Hear the Word of God and Celebrate the Sacraments

God's holy people, *in and as communities,* are nourished by God's word and the sacraments. The right of the Christian faithful to the preaching of the word and the celebration of the sacraments is both basic and communal. "Since the people of God are first brought together by the word of the living God...sacred ministers are to value greatly the task of preaching; among their principal duties is the proclaiming of the gospel of God to all" (c. 762). The Christian faithful have the right to receive assistance from the sacred pastors out of the spiritual goods of the church, especially the word of God and the sacraments (c. 213). This includes the right to worship in the rite (ritual church tradition) to which the members belong (c. 214).

The responsibilities of the pastor of the parish to see that the word of God is well preached and the sacraments devoutly celebrated (c. 528) underline and reinforce the rights of the parish community to these vital sources of spiritual nourishment. What is true of parishes in this regard also applies to other local communities of the faithful.

The right of local communities to the eucharist is a special instance of the more general right to word and sacraments. The eucharistic celebration is at the very heart of the Catholic tradition. The Lord's Supper is a central symbol of our faith and a primary presence of Christ with his people. The eucharist is a sacrament of love, a sign of unity and a bond of charity. The faithful are to participate in it knowingly, actively, devoutly and fruitfully (SC 11, 47, 48). "The Eucharistic Sacrifice...is the summit and source of all Christian worship and life" (c. 897).

For a parish or other local community to be without the regular, weekly, worthy celebration of the eucharist is a most serious deprivation. It is a violation of the community's right to the sacrament in which it finds its own fullest realization and self-expression. It constitutes a grave impoverishment that can gradually deform the community, that is, transform it into one no longer eucharistically centered.

5. Pastoral Leadership and Ministry

The ordinary expectation is that the pastoral care of every parish is entrusted to a priest as its pastor (c. 515.1). In cases of need, the pastoral care may be entrusted to others (cc. 516.2, 517.2), but in either event the community has a right to appropriate pastoral leadership and ministry.

There are canonical standards for this pastoral leadership, and these requirements reveal the implicit ministerial rights of the people of the congregation.

The community should be consulted regarding the selection of its pastor or other ministerial leader. This is not strictly required by the canons, but it is suggested (c. 524), and a proper esteem for communities of the faithful recommends it.

The pastor or pastoral team is to reside within the parish (c. 533), share the lives of the families entrusted to their care, get to know them personally and advise, support and assist them, especially the poor and afflicted among them (c. 529.1). This

nal relationship and rapport with the people is at the heart
of good pastoral care.

The pastor and those who assist him must preach the word of
God, teach the truths of faith (cc. 528.1, 757, 764–771) and see that
catechesis and sacramental preparation is given (cc. 773–777,
843.2). The Christian community is entitled to instruction so that
all can "come to know and live the mystery of salvation" (c. 217).
The teaching office, in its various modes, is a primary ministerial
responsibility (c. 762).

Those in pastoral leadership are "to see to it that the Most Holy
Eucharist is the center of the parish assembly of the faithful," that
the people are nourished by the sacraments and that they actively
participate in the liturgy (cc. 528.2, 835–836, 843.1). The congregation has a strong claim on its ministerial leaders for this spiritual assistance (cc. 213–214).

The local community also has the right to pastoral guidance,
organizational direction and apt administration of its monies,
goods and properties (cc. 519, 532, 1279–1289). The congregation should participate in the pastoral and financial direction of
its affairs through consultation, either directly or by representation. The parish pastoral council and finance council are meant
to be instruments for this consultation (cc. 536–537, 1280).
Pastors are charged to foster lay involvement in the pastoral task,
the parish communion and the church's entire mission
(cc. 519, 529.2).

The community must also contribute materially to meet the
needs of the church, both local and larger (cc. 222, 1262).

Stability in office is another canonical standard for pastors.
The pastoral office implies an enduring relationship with a community of people (c. 522). It takes time as well as effort to know
the people, visit their families and learn their cares. Pastoral leaders are to be a recognized and reliable resource for the lives of
their people, not strangers or visitors in their midst.

6. Initiate and Sustain Activities and Services

Each Catholic congregation expresses itself in distinct modes
of Christian witness and service. The local community initiates,
promotes and sustains apostolic activities, evangelical outreach,
projects for justice and works of charity (cc. 211, 215–216,

298–299, 384.2, 839.1). These are the works that show that the community's faith is truly alive (Jas 2:14–26).

The parish has a duty to promote social justice and to assist the poor (c. 222.2), and it should find its own ways to do so. The community can gather, converse and even form groups and associations for these and other purposes, especially those related to the Christian witness in the world (cc. 215, 225, 227).

7. Information, Communication, Consultation

Parishes and other local Catholic congregations have the right to be informed about those matters that concern them as communities. They are entitled to timely and accurate information, whether about plans and prospects originating from within the community or arising from without, for example, from the diocese.

The Christian faithful, individually and collectively, have the right to make known their needs, desires and opinions to their pastors and to one another (c. 212.2, 212.3). This canonical freedom of expression, which was explicitly declared by the Second Vatican Council (*LG* 37), implies a right to be informed about matters that affect the community. The group cannot form meaningful opinions if they are kept in the dark about the actual situation.

Adequate expression of needs, desires and opinions requires opportunities and channels for communication. These can include meetings, forums, hearings, telephone trees, mailings and access to parish bulletins and other publications.

8. Formation and Education

Every Christian community has the basic need and obligation to form its new members and assist all its members with growing in faith and love (c. 217). Catholic education is a corporate ecclesial duty and right (c. 794).

The stages of catechumenal preparation of adults for initiation into the community and the instruction of parents of infants before their baptism are required in every parish (cc. 851, 788). New members are to be furthered in faith, by both understanding and action, and brought to a greater love for Christ and the church (c. 789). The entire catechumenate process is an essentially communitarian activity.

Parents and pastors and all the Christian faithful share responsibility for the church's educational efforts, including both Catholic schools and suitable education in other ways (cc. 793–798). The duties of sponsorship and support of these efforts are congregational as well as individual (c. 800).

9. Evangelization and Missionary Activity

The church is missionary by its very nature (c. 781). The charge to proclaim the gospel to the nations is foundational to the identity of the church. The command of the Risen Lord is specific: "Go into the whole world and proclaim the gospel to every creature" (Mk 16:15; see also Mt 28:19–20, Lk 24:46–47, Acts 1:8). The basic right and duty rests upon congregations as well as individuals:

> All the Christian faithful have the duty and right to work so that the divine message of salvation may increasingly reach the whole of humankind in every age and in every land. (C. 211)

Vocations to missionary work as well as to the sacred ministry are to be fostered in local communities, and financial assistance for the missions and for seminaries is also to be sought from them (cc. 233, 264, 791).

10. Spiritual Growth

Each parish community must continually attend to its own spiritual condition. It must be concerned with its ongoing repentance, conversion and spiritual growth. "All the Christian faithful must strive...to live a holy life and to promote the growth and continual sanctification of the church" (c. 210). The church to be sanctified is primarily the local church. It is a corporate challenge and a mutual quest (e.g., c. 770).

Various forms and "schools" of the spiritual life are to be provided, to the extent possible. "The Christian faithful have the right...to follow their own form of spiritual life consonant with the teaching of the church" (c. 214). The liturgy of the hours, healthy devotional practices, various prayer forms, veneration of the saints and penitential practices, in keeping with the traditions and desires of the people, are to be encouraged and maintained in local communities (cc. 1174.2, 839, 1186).

11. Own and Use Goods and Property

Parishes and other juridic persons have the right to acquire, retain, administer and dispose of their own goods and property (cc. 1255–1256). They do so in keeping with canonical norms (cc. 1257, 1276), but on their own authority. For this reason each parish must have a finance council (c. 537).

Local congregations of the Catholic faithful possess a legitimate autonomy and responsibility for their monies, investment, buildings, furnishings and property. Dominion over these temporal goods belongs to the parish that purchased or inherited them (c. 1256). These goods are church property and are to be cared for with the diligence of a good householder (cc. 1257, 1284).

12. Vindicate and Defend Rights

Just as individual members of "the Christian faithful can legitimately vindicate and defend the rights which they enjoy in the church before a competent ecclesiastical court" (c. 221.1), so too communities of the faithful have standing to uphold their rights. These local congregations must be judged in accordance with canon law, punished (if that would ever be contemplated) according to the canons and treated with canonical equity (c. 221.2, 221.3).

This canonical standing is obvious in regard to parishes because they enjoy the status of juridic persons by reason of their very establishment (c. 515.3). But other local Catholic congregations, which do not have the canonical status of parishes, should be accorded rights and held to obligations as parishes are. These other local communities are recognized in the Code (e.g., cc. 516, 556–563, 564–572, 813), and equity requires that they receive similar treatment.

The specific ways in which parish rights and duties can be vindicated or defended will be treated in the next chapter.

Limitations on Rights and Obligations

Rights and duties are not absolute. They are conditioned or limited in at least three ways: (1) by circumstances, (2) by the rights of others and (3) by the common good.

1. Rights and duties are not exercised in a vacuum. Parishes and other local congregations exist in the real world. They must recognize and operate within the limits of concrete situations. Resources of personnel, time and money are limited; sometimes they can be stretched no further. No one should expect the impossible.

2. The prerogatives of one parish or community cannot be advanced to the detriment of others. A sense of balance, fairness and respect for rights must characterize the claims of each.

3. The principle of the common good governs rights claims and the demands of obligations. It calls for coordination. All of the communities within a diocese "have a place at the table." All must be heard from and accounted for, and each one must show consideration for the rest and for the good of the entire church.

> In exercising their rights the Christian faithful, both as individuals and when gathered in associations, must take account of the common good of the church, and of the rights of others as well as their own duties towards others.
>
> In the interests of the common good, church authority has competence to regulate the exercise of the rights which belong to the Christian faithful. (C. 223.1, 223.2)

Listing canonical parish rights and obligations is not an exercise in legalism. The intention is not to promote litigation or to reduce ecclesial communion to a juridical battlefield where adversarial fights about rights take place.

Listing canonical rights and obligations helps to portray the dignity of the local church. It is one way of coloring in the authentic character of local congregations of the Catholic faithful. Parishes are not administrative units of some larger entity. They are true churches. They should see themselves as such, and be accorded the respect due to churches.

The following chapter will explore options in the event that parish rights and obligations are neglected or violated.

Sources and Readings

Refer to the Code of Canon Law and its commentaries cited at the end of Chapter 5.

7
Claiming Parish Rights

The previous chapter asserted that communities of the faithful, that is, parishes and other local congregations, possess both rights and obligations within the church. Two questions now arise: who can claim these rights, and how can they do so? These are the two questions to be addressed in this chapter: who can vindicate the rights and press the obligations of local communities of the Catholic faithful, and what are the means by which they can do so? Before responding to these two questions, it is important to recall the relationship between parishes and dioceses.

The Parish and the Diocese

The bold assertion of the rights and obligations of Catholic parishes and other local congregations is based squarely on the theological fact that these groupings constitute the primary reality of the church. The Roman Catholic Church worldwide is a communion of particular churches, that is, of diocesan churches, each led by a bishop, who is a member of the College of Bishops. Each diocesan church, in turn, is a communion of local churches, mainly parishes. But the parishes and other local congregations are where the people are, where the faithful actually live and interact as church. (Even when some of them reside elsewhere, they come together as church in local parishes.)

Those who have been fully incorporated into the church know and relate to one another as Christians in local communities. They are reborn into Christ and are nourished into Christian

82

maturity in their local churches. It is there that they care for one another, grow and develop together, worship and witness together. The church exists first and foremost in its stable local congregations of the faithful.

Parishes and other local congregations are not like the branch offices or local outlets of a central corporation, as local banks or auto agencies or service stations often are. They are unique communities of Christian people. They are authentic churches, just like those described in the New Testament (in Jerusalem, in Antioch, in Corinth, in Ephesus), and they must be respected as such. The church is built up from below by these local communities of God's people.

Parishes represent far more than a convenient way of dividing up and administering a diocesan church. Parishes constitute the church's first level of reality, and dioceses are administrative units. The bishop, who is an overseer, a superintendent and a spokesperson, is to guide, assist and support these local congregations. The diocesan bishop and those who work with him at the diocesan level of church are to serve and coordinate the parishes and other local communities within their territory. Dioceses exist to unify and enable the local churches.

People enter the church, grow in faith, give praise to God and lend loving assistance to their neighbors in parishes and other local communities. These local congregations of the faithful have a proper and authentic autonomy that must be respected.

One of the ways in which this legitimate autonomy is spelled out, explained and circumscribed is in terms of the rights and obligations of parishes. Sometimes it appears as though parish rights and duties are not taken seriously, not honored. That is when the issue of vindication of rights arises. The Code of Canon Law speaks of the "vindication and defense" of the rights of the Christian faithful (c. 221.1).

The term *to vindicate* (from the Latin *vindicare*, to claim or set free), does not mean to win or to conquer; it does not carry a combative or litigious overtone. It means to assert a right, to make it good, to act in one's own interest, to defend against encroachment or interference. The expression does not have the sense of getting even or settling scores but of claiming legitimate interests or prerogatives. When there is a perception that the rights of a parish have been violated or that the parish community has failed in one of its obligations, who can vindicate that right or enforce that obligation? It is a question of agency and of equity. The answers are multiple and varied, depending on the pastoral leadership situation.

Those Who Can Claim Parish Rights

1. The Pastor of the Parish and His Substitutes

"The pastor represents the parish in all juridic affairs in accord with the norm of law" (c. 532). It is incumbent upon the pastor, by reason of his office, to pursue the canonical rights and duties of the community whose pastoral care has been entrusted to him. He is to be vigilant on behalf of his people, safeguarding their legitimate interests and urging their responsibilities. The pastor is not at liberty to permit the rights of the congregation to be violated or abridged, even by those in higher authority. Likewise, he is to call upon the parish community to shoulder its rightful obligations.

A parochial administrator who is appointed to substitute for a pastor is bound by the same duties as the pastor (c. 540.1). Likewise, the parochial vicar (assistant pastor) who assumes the governance of the parish until an administrator is appointed bears those same responsibilities (c. 541). And the priest placed in charge of a quasi-parish (c. 516) has similar responsibilities to those of a pastor. All of these persons are required to urge the rights and obligations of the communities entrusted to them.

2. Those Entrusted with the Pastoral Care of the Parish

Deacons, religious brothers or sisters, lay men or women, or a community of such persons may be given the pastoral charge of a parish community (c. 517.2). In those arrangements, the person or persons to whom the pastoral care has been entrusted must see to the rights and obligations of the parish community. The priest moderator (or supervisor), who is endowed with the powers and faculties of pastor and oversees those entrusted with the pastoral care of the parish, has a residual and secondary duty to pursue the rights of the parish. But the ministerial leader of the parish community, who is the one in charge on the scene and has a personal and pastoral relationship with the members of the community, bears the primary responsibility.

3. The Parish Pastoral Council and Finance Council

In the event that the pastor or his substitute or those entrusted with the pastoral care of the parish cannot or will not act to vindicate or defend the rights of the parish community, the obvious agent for the parish is the pastoral council. The council's main role is to help foster the pastoral activity of the parish (c. 536). It is to assist the pastor and other pastoral leaders, but it also represents the parish community in a real sense. In the event that the pastor or other ministerial leaders are absent, impeded or unwilling to act in furtherance of the rights of the parish, the pastoral council may take such action. Indeed, in certain circumstances the council may be obliged to act on behalf of the parish community. The same is true of the canonically required finance council for issues related to parish property and funds (c. 537).

4. Parishioners

Individual members of the parish community have an obvious interest in and a responsibility for the rights and obligations of the parish. Do they have standing "to vindicate and defend" the rights of the parish as juridic person? They are not canonically designated as, nor usually considered to be, the representatives of a parish (that is, the parish *as* a juridic person, cc. 118, 532). Yet, they not only have an interest in the welfare of their parish community, but they can suffer real harm from, for example, the suppression of their parish or destruction of the parish church. Hence their capacity for action or their legal standing is based on a subjective right or legitimate interest in their parish, an interest that is personal, direct, actual and founded on canonical provisions. (The canonical provisions are the canons of the Code that incorporate them as members of the parish, either territorial or personal, cc. 102, 518, or their de facto acceptance as parish members, which entitles them to pastoral care.)

A large group of parishioners represents the parish community more appropriately than do a few individuals. For instance, a majority or a very large minority of those who belong to the parish usually constitutes a truly representative group. However, the Apostolic Signatura (the supreme court of the Catholic Church) has recognized as few as two parishioners to have standing to pursue an appeal against a decree of suppression of their parish. The supreme tribunal based its decision on the vital interest that each member has in the parish community (Prot. No. 22036/90 C.A., *Chicagien., Suppressionis paroeciae*, D.mi Anzelmo et Ciambrone vs. Congr. pro Clericis; decision given June 20, 1992).

5. *Those Outside the Parish Community*

Church officials and councils with duties related to parishes have at least a residual responsibility to see to the defense of the rights and fulfillment of obligations of the parishes within their areas of authority. Deans have such duties within their deanery or vicariate (c. 555). Episcopal vicars, who have authority for parishes in the entire diocese or within a determined section of the diocese (c. 476), must also attend to the rights and duties of parishes.

The presbyteral council (priests' senate), which has both general (c. 495.1) and specific canonical responsibilities in regard to parishes (c. 515.2, 1222.2), must attend carefully to their welfare.

When claims involving parish rights come before the diocesan tribunal, the promoter of justice, who is bound to provide for the public good (c. 1430), should intervene.

Finally, both the diocesan bishop and his vicar general are obliged to look after the legitimate rights and duties of the parishes within the diocese (cc. 384, 391–394, 396, 475; *Directory on the Pastoral Ministry of Bishops*, 174–183).

The above persons and groups have, at least in default of actions by other more immediately responsible persons, the duty to act in defense or vindication of the rights of parishes. But *how* can they do so? What are the means by which the rights and obligations of parish communities can be pursued?

How the Rights of Parishes Can Be Vindicated

4 Lines
of Action

There are at least four lines of action that those charged with the defense of parish rights can pursue: (1) be alert and participate in information-gathering and decision-making processes in advance of any action against the interests of the parish, (2) after the fact, seek a solution through direct appeal, conciliation or mediation, (3) take administrative recourse against an action that is perceived to be adverse to parish rights and (4) bring the matter before an ecclesiastical court.

These four steps prescind from and, if successful, would obviate public demonstrations, letter writing campaigns, attempts at newspaper or television publicity or recourse to civil courts. These regrettable alternatives are frequently resorted to when procedures within the church are not available or are unsuccessful. They call to mind St. Paul's admonition to the Corinthians: "Can it be that there is not one among you wise enough to be able to settle a case between brothers [or sisters]?" (see 1 Cor 6:5–6).

1. Engagement and Awareness

Those who represent the parish and care about its life and activities must be fully engaged in whatever studies, plans, reviews or assessments involve the parish. Actions that affect parish communities often result from investigations or information gathering projects, whether initiated from within the parish or by agencies of the diocese. Sometimes great harm is caused by lack of awareness that such processes are under way or by failing to take them seriously. Responsible leaders, staff and members of the parish must participate fully and persistently in all phases of such activity. Accurate data, solid evidence and persuasive arguments must be presented in a timely manner. Those within the parish must be kept well informed, and the progress of such investigations must be carefully and patiently monitored.

2. Direct Appeal, Conciliation or Mediation

After some action has been taken that is perceived to be contrary to the rights of the parish community, that is, that appears to harm or adversely affect that community, the first attempts should be direct, personal and low-key. ("If your brother [or sister] sins against you, go and tell him his fault between you and him alone. If he listens to you, you have won over your brother" [Mt 18:15].) Conversations should be initiated that present the parish's point of view, show the evidence and muster the arguments on behalf of the interests of the parish. The point (as canon 1733.1 states) is to avoid contention and controversy between the aggrieved party (in this case the parish community) and the author of the action. The Christian mandate is to preserve the bonds of charity that tie church communities together.

If other wisdom is needed, for example, a facilitator of conciliation, a mediator or even an arbitrator, let such a person be brought in so that a just and equitable solution can be found. This avoidance of disputes and litigation is an insistent canonical mandate, and effective means to accomplish it should be available within the diocesan church (cc. 1733, 1446, 1713–1716). Such due process offices do function in many dioceses.

3. Administrative Recourse

The procedure for appealing an administrative decision to the author of the decision or to that person's hierarchical superior is outlined in canons 1732–1739 of the Code. Since the Catholic Church is very hierarchically structured, this process is often effective in the sense that it gives access to the persons who have the ability to make a difference (see c. 1739).

The first step of the process is an appeal in writing to the one who made the decision, that is, to the administrator who took the action that is perceived to be harmful to the community (c. 1734.1). The second step, which may be taken "for any just reason," is an appeal to the hierarchical superior of the one who took the action (c. 1737), for example, from a pastor to the diocesan bishop, or from a school principal to the superintendent of schools or from a diocesan bishop to the Congregation for the Clergy in Rome.

The canons state specific time-terms within which the appeals must be lodged (e.g., ten working days for the first appeal), and they provide for the suspension of the action while the appeal is being considered.

A possible third step (if, for example, the first was an appeal to the diocesan bishop, and the second to the Congregation for the Clergy in Rome) in this process of administrative appeal is recourse to the supreme tribunal of the Apostolic Signatura. The second section of the Signatura has authority to review administrative decisions (c. 1445.2).

(Appeals to the congregations or tribunals of the Holy See may be made directly or through the official representative of the Holy See. In the United States that person is the apostolic pro-nuncio in Washington, 3339 Massachusetts Ave., N.W., Washington, D.C., 20008. Addresses and officials of the Roman Curia can be found in *The Official Catholic Directory* published annually by P. J. Kenedy & Sons, New York.)

It should be noted that administrative appeals to hierarchical superiors fly in the face of the principle of subsidiarity and inevitably contribute to the centralization of authority in the church. For that reason they should be made neither lightly nor casually but only as a last resort.

The principle of subsidiary function is a central teaching of the church's modern social encyclicals. It calls for decisions to be taken and conflicts to be resolved as close to the human person and local community as possible.

4. Ecclesiastical Courts

Canon 221, in the section of the Code on the obligations and rights of all the Christian faithful, solemnly declares that "the Christian faithful can legitimately vindicate and defend the rights which they enjoy in the Church before a competent ecclesiastical court in accord with the norms of law." Access to the church's courts is reiterated in canon 1491: "Every right whatsoever is safe-guarded not only by an action (i.e., the request of a petitioner) but also by an exception (i.e., the claim of a defendant) unless something to the contrary is expressly stated." This standing to vindicate and defend rights applies to juridic persons, such as parishes, as well as to physical persons.

The provision of canon 1400.2, which states that "controver-sies which have arisen from an act of administrative power can be brought only before the superior or an administrative tribunal," limits access to church courts in some matters involving adminis-trative decisions but does not bar it entirely. Many actions and conditions that impinge negatively on the rights of parishes are not the direct result of "acts of administrative power." Hence, if a cause of action can be found, for example, negligence, arbitrari-ness, criminal activity, malfeasance, conflict of interests, etc., then the church courts should be open to the parish's claim.

Indeed, the courts exist "to pursue or to vindicate the rights of physical or juridic persons" (c. 1400.1).

It is well known that most ecclesiastical courts only judge marriage cases. That is, their entire docket is filled with petitions for the declaration of the juridic status of persons, namely, whether a petitioner is canonically married or unmarried. In other words, virtually all the diocesan courts do is marriage annulments. However, the church's canons (just cited) prescribe that the courts are open to a much wider range of rights claims. Those seeking to pursue the rights of a parish should weigh the possibility of submitting a petition to the diocesan court (cc. 1502–1504).

Every diocese has an ecclesiastical court. It is sometimes referred to as "the court of first instance" (i.e., first level or trial court; cc. 1419–1437). There is an appellate procedure within the system of church courts that involves appeals from the diocesan tribunal to "the court of second instance" of the ecclesiastical province or region, and from there to the Roman Rota (the ordinary court of appeal) at the Holy See, that is, the Vatican (cc. 1438ff., 1628ff., 1442ff.). However, at least in theory, any case at any point of its development may be brought to the Holy See (c. 1417).

In Conclusion

This chapter has attempted to answer this twofold question: who must look out for the rights and duties of parishes and other local communities of the Catholic faithful, and how can they do so?

A healthy respect for the rights and obligations of parishes is one way of highlighting the dignity and priority of this level of the church's existence. Parishes are where the people live; their lives of faith and their interaction in local communities constitute the vitality of the church. These local communities have a legitimate autonomy. It is certainly not absolute, but it commands respect.

The assertion of parish rights and their vindication does not detract from hierarchical authority or the principle of commu-

nion in any way. Rather it emphasizes the communitarian principle within the church and focuses on the church's true nature as
a communion of local communities. It is an authentic expression
of the Catholic tradition.

Sources and Readings

In addition to those canonical publications cited at the end of
Chapter 5:

Congregation for Bishops. *Directory on the Pastoral Ministry of
Bishops,* May 31, 1973. Ottawa: Canadian Catholic Conference,
1974.

Diocesan Efforts at Parish Reorganization. Clearwater, Fla.:
Conference for Pastoral Planning and Council Development,
1995.

John Paul II. Apostolic Constitution *Pastor Bonus* (on the Roman
Curia), June 28, 1988. Published as an appendix in *Code of
Canon Law Annotated.* Montreal: Wilson & Lafleur Ltd., 1993,
pp. 1166–1279.

The Official Catholic Directory. New York: P.J. Kenedy & Sons, published annually.

Protection of Rights of Persons in the Church. Revised Report of the
Canon Law Society of America on the Subject of Due Process.
Washington, D.C.: CLSA, 1991.

8
Pastoral Ministry in the Parish

The parish community itself is the primary reality. For that reason the previous chapters have traced the origins of local churches in the New Testament, their development through history, their theological nature and their canonical status. The local community itself is of first importance, then comes the pastoral ministry within the community.

The pastoral ministry within the parish is the community's responsibility. Even though a pastor and others associated with him direct and provide much of the pastoral care, it remains a basic duty of the whole parish community to see that it is provided adequately and supported appropriately. The parish community cannot simply wash its hands of the ministerial responsibilities and leave them to one or a few officeholders.

Pope John Paul II took this notion one step further in a December 18, 1986, address to bishops: "The parish itself is the *active subject of pastoral action*" (John Paul's emphasis). The members of the parish community, in virtue of their baptism, confirmation and common priesthood, acting in solidarity, are the united subject of pastoral action. "It is the parish which renders the mystery of the Church and of its mission living and operative."

For a very long time in the Catholic tradition it was the other way around. The priest-pastor was in central focus. Canon law centered on his duties, his rights, his tenure, his income. The community was the people he served, but it seemed more like the stage on which he acted, the territory entrusted to him. The priest-pastor appeared to be the factotum, the one who did everything. He alone did the ministering in the parish, or so it seemed, and everyone else was relatively passive.

That is certainly not true any more, as everyone knows. Ministry is now widely shared within the parish community. Many persons play very active roles in the parish, just as they did in the early church. (St. Paul wrote about lists of leaders and their functions; see Chapter 2.) Professional staff, both religious and lay, are very common now, and the number of volunteer ministers of various kinds is nothing short of phenomenal. Many persons contribute to the pastoral care given in most American parishes today.

This proliferation and distribution of pastoral roles resulted principally from the active involvement of lay Catholics rather than from a shortage of priests. Laity and religious have responded in large numbers to the invitation and encouragement that the Second Vatican Council gave to their active participation in every facet of the life of their local community and its ministry.

Pastoral Care

Canon law does not yet fully reflect the extent of shared ministry within parishes. The canons still focus on the roles of the pastor, the assistant ("parochial vicar") and the one who substitutes for the pastor in time of incapacity or ill health ("parochial administrator"). However, the canons recognize the participative nature of parish ministry, for instance, in the definition of the pastor's role:

B. S.

> The parish priest is the proper pastor of the parish assigned to him. He exercises pastoral care in the community entrusted to him, under the authority of the diocesan bishop in whose ministry of Christ he has been called to share;...he carries out the duties of teaching, sanctifying, and governing for his community, with the cooperation of other priests or deacons and with the assistance of lay members of the Christian faithful. (C. 519)

Pastoring is a collaborative task. The pastor is obliged to offer pastoral care within the community with the help of others, and in doing so he is subject to the direction of the bishop. His is the primary and central role in the parish's ministry, but it is not separated from the community, nor is it exercised alone. The pastoral task remains collaborative when it is undertaken by laypersons or deacons in the absence of priests.

The Elements of Pastoral Care

Canon law most often assigns responsibility to the parish pastor (or the one who takes his place) for the various elements of pastoral care in the community. This is so for historical reasons and in order to place pastoral accountability on a particular, identifiable person, that is, one who can be held accountable. However, as noted above, the parish community itself is the "active subject of pastoral action" and is ultimately accountable for these five categories of pastoral activity.

1. Ministry of the Word of God

The proclamation and explanation of God's holy word is the first and foremost pastoral duty. The pastor is to see to it that the word of God is announced to those who live in the parish, those who come to church and those who do not. This is to be accomplished through homilies, instructions in the truths of faith, catechetical formation, works that promote the spirit of the gospel and social justice, education of children and of young adults, outreach to those who have ceased practicing their faith as well as the evangelization of those who do not yet believe (c. 528.1).

The pastor is to see to it that God's word is proclaimed, but this preeminent and multifold work itself belongs to many: the lay Christian faithful, parents, catechists, teachers, religious women and men, deacons and other priests (cc. 757–759).

2. Ministry of the Sacred Liturgy

The eucharist is to be the center of the parish congregation, the heart of its gatherings. That is to say, Sunday mass is to be the paramount event of the community's life, its supreme act of worship; the people are to participate in it actively and prayerfully and are to be nourished by communion at the Lord's table. The pastor is to see to it that the other sacraments and liturgical actions, especially penance, are celebrated fruitfully and frequently. Family prayer is to be warmly encouraged (c. 528.2).

The eucharistic sacrifice is the summit and source of all Christian life as well as worship, so the parish community is to foster a eucharistic spirituality that flows over into the lives and activities of its members (c. 897). The parish family is earnestly invited also to celebrate the liturgy of the hours (c. 1174.2).

It goes without saying that the entire parish community is actively engaged in this ministry. Everyone participates, responds, sings, prays and communicates at mass. Many plan and prepare liturgies, sing in choirs, act as welcomers and ushers, serve at the altar, read the scriptures and lead the song.

3. Ministry of Pastoral Charity

The pastor and those who assist him are to strive to know the people of the parish and to visit their families. They are to share the people's cares, worries and griefs and try to strengthen them in the Lord. They sometimes need to correct carefully those who have erred. They are to help the sick, especially those near death, comforting them with the sacraments and commending their souls to God. They are to seek out and assist those who are poor, afflicted, lonely, exiled or otherwise specially burdened. And they are to seek support for parents in rearing their children and help families to grow as Christians (c. 529.1).

Many in the parish community share in this ministry also: those who visit homes and welcome new parishioners, those who take holy communion to those in nursing homes and hospitals, those who counsel troubled individuals and families, those who assist the poor and homeless, and those who reach out to the separated, divorced or widowed.

4. Ministry of Christian Witness

Parishes initiate, support and carry on works of Christian witness. Both as individuals and in groups, parishioners show forth their faith and convictions in works of charity, education, peace and justice, neighborhood or city involvement, ecumenical cooperation, environmental issues and other causes. The parish ministry is to encourage and foster such activities of Christian witness, especially through associations, societies and coalitions founded for such purposes (cc. 529.2, 225, 227, 298).

Parishes relate to and influence their surrounding communities by such concerted efforts and, in doing so, give clear and resounding witness to the beliefs and values that they hold. Local congregations thus give testimony to Christ by showing concern and being of service to those around them.

5. Ministry of Coordination and Administration

The parish communion needs to be built up and solidified, ordered and guided. This is another serious and complex pastoral task. The pastor and those who advise and assist him have responsibility for maintaining the parish ministries and activities and for seeing that they work together in some sort of reasonable Christian harmony. The Christian faithful and those sharing in the pastoral care of the parish are to assist the pastor in fostering and coordinating pastoral activity through the parish council (c. 536).

Those in pastoral leadership must also care responsibly for the property, buildings, funds and resources of the parish. The pastor represents the juridic person of the parish in canonical affairs, and he must see to it that the goods of the parish are administered according to the canons (c. 532). A finance council helps the pastor with the administration of parish goods (c. 537).

The Organization of Parish Ministries

The organizational chart of American Catholic parishes was once standard and predictable. It differed only because of the size of the parish and the number of priests and sisters who were in charge of the various ministries. There was a lot of lay activity, but it wasn't called ministry, and it was very much under clerical direction.

Now there is great variety in the ways that parishes are staffed and in the ways that ministries are organized. This variety has developed out of necessity, for example, to supply for fewer priests and sisters and to meet the higher expectations of parishioners. And the growing number of professionally qualified lay ministers has played a large part. But the reorganization of parish ministry was also facilitated by a few modifications in the church's canon law.

The pastor remains at the center of parish ministry. His role is included in the opening canon on parishes: "The pastoral care of the parish is entrusted to a parish priest as its own pastor" (c. 515). Subsequent canons ascribe many duties and prerogatives to the pastor. A pastor for every parish is still the canonical norm, as it has been since the time of Charlemagne.

However, the pastor's ministry is now described in collaborative terms, as was mentioned above. The canons direct or imply that others—laypersons, deacons, religious, assisting priests—will work with the pastor in providing pastoral care (cc. 519, 528–529, 536–537, 545–548).

In addition, the revised Code of 1983 provides for a new variety of alternatives to the usual one-priest-pastor-for-each-parish paradigm:

1. When circumstances require it, rather than assigning a pastor to a parish, the parish or even several parishes can be entrusted to a team of priests who share in exercising pastoral care; one is designated as the moderator of the team (c. 517.1).

2. The pastoral care of a parish may be entrusted to a deacon, a layperson, or a religious sister or brother (or a community of such persons); a priest elsewhere with a pastor's authority is named to moderate them (c. 517.2). The diocesan bishop may authorize this arrangement when there is a shortage of priests. Such non-priest parish leaders may be empowered to do everything that a priest-pastor does in the parish and its ministries, except those things that require priestly ordination, that is, presiding at the eucharist, hearing confessions, confirming and anointing the sick (cc. 129.2, 230.3).

3. The care of several neighboring parishes may be entrusted to one pastor, if necessary, because of a shortage of priests or other reasons (c. 526.1).

4. Parochial vicars (assistant priests) may be assigned to one or to several parishes. They may minister in one part of a parish, be in charge of some ministries within the entire parish or perform certain ministries in a number of parishes (c. 545).

5. Quasi-parishes, chaplaincies, missions, pastoral centers and

a variety of "other arrangements" besides parishes may be established by the diocesan bishop to meet the spiritual needs of special groups of people (cc. 516, 556, 564, 813). In other words, there are a range of possibilities, in addition to parishes, to provide for the pastoral care of local churches and the ministries within them.

6. Within parishes or other communities laypersons may be asked, when it is necessary or when ministers are lacking, to perform many ministries that do not require priestly ordination. These include preaching, catechizing, presiding at liturgical prayers, conferring baptism, distributing holy communion, assisting at marriages, conducting funerals, counseling, visiting the sick, administering parish goods, keeping sacramental records, etc. (cc. 129.2, 230.3, 759, 766, 776, 1112).

It is obvious from this brief survey that a wide variety of canonical possibilities exists for organizing and delivering pastoral care in parishes. Initiatives in the actual practice of ministry are daily expanding these possibilities.

The Second Vatican Council decreed that "the whole purpose of the parish is the good of souls" (*CD* 31). The most important consideration in organizing the pastoral care in a parish or other local congregation is to provide for the spiritual welfare of the people.

Pope John Paul II, in his 1988 *Apostolic Exhortation on the Laity,* repeated the words of the bishops at the 1987 synod with regard to parishes with special challenges, such as urban change, lack of resources, lack of ordained ministers or an influx of immigrants. He made these suggestions about the organization of such parishes:

> So that all parishes of this kind may be truly communities of Christians, local ecclesial authorities ought to foster the following: (a) adaptation of parish structures according to the full flexibility granted by canon law, especially in promoting participation by the lay faithful in pastoral responsibilities; (b) small, basic or so-called "living" communities where the faithful can communicate the word of God and express it in service and love to one another; these communities are true expressions of ecclesial communion and centers of evangelization in communion with their pastors. (*CL* 26)

Whatever is the organization of the parish and its ministries, pastoral care must be exercised with mutual respect and close collaboration between laypersons and ordained ministers if the people are to be well served.

Sources and Readings

About ministry:

Bausch, W. *Ministry: Traditions, Tensions, Transitions.* Mystic, Conn.: Twenty-Third Publications, 1982.

Bernier, P. *Ministry in the Church: A Historical and Pastoral Approach.* Mystic, Conn.: Twenty-Third Publications, 1992.

Cooke, B. *Ministry to Word and Sacrament: History and Theology.* Philadelphia: Fortress, 1976.

Lynch, J. "The Parochial Ministry in the New Code of Canon Law." *Jurist* 42, 2 (1982): 383–421.

McBrien, R. *Ministry: A Theological, Pastoral Handbook.* San Francisco: Harper & Row, 1987.

O'Meara, T. *Theology of Ministry.* New York: Paulist Press, 1983.

Osborne, K. *Ministry: Lay Ministry in the Roman Catholic Church: Its History and Theology.* Mahwah, N.J.: Paulist Press, 1993.

Schillebeeckx, E. *The Church with a Human Face: A New and Expanded Theology of Ministry.* London: SCM Press, 1985.

A Shepherd's Care: Reflections on the Changing Role of Pastor. Bishops' Committee on Priestly Life and Ministry, NCCB. Washington, D.C.: USCC, 1987.

About parish:

Bausch, W. *The Christian Parish: Whispers of the Risen Christ.* Mystic, Conn.: Twenty-Third Publications, 1980.

————. *The Total Parish Manual: Everything You Need to Empower Your Faith Community.* Mystic, Conn.: Twenty-Third Publications, 1994.

Brennan, P. *Parishes That Excel: Models of Excellence in Education, Ministry, and Evangelization.* New York: Crossroad, 1992.

—————. *Re-imagining the Parish: Base Communities, Adulthood, and Family Consciousness.* New York: Crossroad, 1990.

Castelli, J., and J. Gremillion. *The Emerging Parish: The Notre Dame Study of Catholic Life since Vatican II.* San Francisco: Harper & Row, 1987.

Cusack, B., and T. Sullivan. *Pastoral Care in Parishes Without a Pastor.* Washington, D.C.: CLSA, 1995.

DeSiano, F., and K. Boyack. *Creating the Evangelizing Parish.* Mahwah, N.J.: Paulist Press, 1995.

Foley, G. *Family-Centered Church: A New Model.* Kansas City: Sheed & Ward, 1995.

Murnion, P., et al. *New Parish Ministers: Laity & Religious on Parish Staffs.* New York: National Pastoral Life Center, 1992.

—————. "The Parish of the Future." *Church* 12, 1 (Spring 1996): 5–10.

National Pastoral Life Center. "Alternate Staffing of Parishes." Center Paper No. 3, Spring, 1987. New York.

O'Brien, J., ed. *Gathering God's People: Signs of a Successful Parish.* Huntington, Ind.: Our Sunday Visitor, 1982.

Searle, M., ed. *Parish: A Place for Worship.* Collegeville, Minn.: Liturgical Press, 1980.

Sofield, L., and B. Hermann. *Developing the Parish As a Community of Service.* New York: LeJacq Publications, 1984.

Sweetser, T. *Successful Parishes: How They Meet the Challenge of Change.* Minneapolis: Winston, 1983.

Sweetser, T., and P. Forster. *Transforming the Parish: Models for the Future.* Kansas City: Sheed & Ward, 1993.

Sweetser, T., and C. Holden. *Leadership in a Successful Parish.* San Francisco: Harper & Row, 1987.

U.S. Bishops' Committee on the Parish. "The Parish: A People, a Mission, a Structure." *Origins* 10, 41 (March 26, 1981): 641–46.

Wallace, R. *They Call Her Pastor: A New Role for Catholic Women.* Albany: State University of New York, 1992.

Whitehead, E., ed. *The Parish in Commmunity and Ministry.* New York: Paulist Press, 1978.

9
Parish Relationships

Parishes, like all human communities, do not exist in a vacuum. They live among other communities, and they interact with them. This chapter is a brief reflection on those relationships. It does not treat of the relationships between the parishioners and their ministers, or among the parishioners themselves, but rather of the relationships between the parish as a community and other communities.

There are at least five categories of parish relationships: (1) to the diocese, (2) to the nearby Catholic parishes and communities, (3) to more distant Catholic communities, (4) to local Protestant, Jewish and other religious communities and (5) to neighborhood, civic and political communities.

Parish and Diocese

Each parish is a part of a diocese. Each is a community within the family of communities that makes up the diocesan communion. It is mainly through the diocese that each parish is linked to the worldwide communion that is called the Catholic Church. The canons of the Code of Canon Law describe a diocese this way:

> A diocese is that portion of the people of God which is entrusted for pastoral care to a bishop with the cooperation of the presbyterate. It adheres to him, its pastor, and is gathered together by him in the Holy Spirit, through the Gospel and the Eucharist. A diocese constitutes a particular church in which the one, holy, catholic and apostolic Church of Christ exists and functions. (C. 369)

101

The universal Church is built up out of these particular churches called dioceses. (C. 368)

Each local parish must maintain close bonds of communion with its diocese and the other local churches that make it up. This solemn obligation to respect and maintain communion is rooted in the very identity of the parish as a local Catholic church.

The bonds of communion are the profession of a common faith, the celebration of the sacraments and obedience to the church's authority (cc. 205, 209). These principles of communion come down to practice in the parish's relationship to the diocese and its bishop (cc. 386–387, 391–392, 394).

Communion also implies material support, so that the diocesan church can assist local churches with greater resources and expertise than they themselves could afford (c. 222). The diocesan bishop can levy a tax on parishes, proportionate to their means, to pay for such diocesan needs (c. 1263).

The relationship between the parish and the diocese is not one of inferior to superior. Nor is it one of subservience and dominion. It is a reciprocal relationship of support and assistance, a mutual relationship of respect and care. The diocesan communion of local churches is an administrative unit that manifests and maintains the unity among those churches and lends help to them in a variety of ways.

The diocese often provides administrative assistance for schools, resources for religious education, counseling services for individuals and families, financial assistance, continuing education for priests and other ministers, liturgical guidance, marriage preparation programs and a marriage tribunal. Dioceses also provide various forms of direct ministry. Diocesan personnel and agencies, often referred to as "the chancery" or "the pastoral center," assist the bishop in his responsibilities to promote the common discipline of the church and to foster and coordinate the works of the apostolate (cc. 392, 394).

The diocesan bishop is obliged to make a canonical visitation, either personally or through a delegate, to each one of the parishes in the diocese at least every five years (c. 396). This periodic pastoral check-up visit is another important sign of communion between the diocese and the parish.

Each pastor has the duty to help the parish community realize its membership in and responsibilities for the diocese (c. 529.2).

The pastor is one symbol of this connection to the diocesan church. He is assigned to the parish as pastor by the bishop and carries out his duties under the bishop's authority (cc. 515.1, 519, 523). Obviously, this is true also of those who exercise pastoral leadership in parishes but who are not ordained. They too embody the parish's close and multifaceted relationship with the diocese, even though they do not share with the bishop the sacrament of holy orders as a priest-pastor does.

At every celebration of the eucharist the parish community is reminded that it is a part of something larger than itself, something called the communion of saints. The parish at worship is connected historically with the apostles, martyrs and saints of old. It is connected with other worshiping communities around the world. And it is connected with the communion of other local churches that make up the diocese under the leadership of the bishop. The bishop is named and prayed for at every mass as a daily sign of the parish's participation in the diocesan communion.

Parish and Deanery or Vicariate

Parishes and other local communities of the faithful relate to the other parishes in their neighborhood, their section of town or city, or their county or part of the state, in loose associations known as deaneries or vicariates. These organizational districts, headed by a dean, an episcopal vicar or an auxiliary bishop, exist to coordinate pastoral activity locally and to provide some surveillance over the churches and their ministers within areas of the diocese (cc. 476, 479, 555). These regional groupings of local churches are not as important as the diocesan communion is. However, they are another real expression of the communion of local churches and of their unity and collaboration in mission. Parishes, even though they possess considerable legitimate autonomy, do not exist or function in isolation. Being a part of a communion implies mutual assistance and friendly cooperation.

The regular meetings of the pastors and other ministers from the adjacent parishes is a valuable occasion for exchange of information and coordination of activities. These gatherings are important opportunities for consultation on matters of policy as well.

Sometimes neighboring parishes join together in long-term projects, such as sponsoring a regional high school, counseling center, soup kitchen or shelter for the homeless. They are able to do together what no one of them could do alone.

Parish-to-Parish Connections

When parishes enter into partnerships with other parishes at greater distance, it often promotes remarkable and far-reaching results. For example, a suburban or rural parish might enter into a covenant with an urban or inner-city parish. Or a North American parish might engage in a long-term agreement with a parish or mission in Central or South America. These arrangements are sometimes called pairing or twinning.

Such parish-to-parish connections are based on mutual needs and assistance, but more deeply they are based on Christian love and the sense of solidarity within the churches of the Catholic communion. Most often they link more affluent churches with those in relative poverty.

This sharing of resources is precisely what St. Paul warmly encouraged among the churches in the first century. He spoke of genuine love manifested in generosity and practical assistance, that is, a collection for the church in Jerusalem (see 1 Cor 16:1–4 and 2 Cor 8).

Ongoing exchanges such as these between communities encourage personal contacts and group interaction as well as charitable assistance, and the results are often transcendent. Families and parish groups exchange visits, sponsor joint programs and encourage communication and friendships. This pattern of activity is especially meaningful when it occurs across racial, ethnic or national lines.

The experience of this kind of outreach can transform communities on both sides. It helps to lift both congregations out of a narrow parochialism; it raises the vision and involvements of both communities to a higher level of Christian awareness and engagement.

Ecumenical Relationships

The Second Vatican Council moved the Catholic Church into the mainstream of both the ecumenical movement and interreligious dialogue and cooperation. The ecumenical movement works for better understanding and eventual unity among Christians. The interreligious movement promotes Christian cooperation with those of Jewish, Islamic and other faith traditions. In both cases, community engagement is more powerful and effective than merely personal or even ministerial efforts.

Catholic parishes once gave the cold shoulder to their neighboring Protestant congregations. No more. The former mutual reserve, sometimes bordering on animosity, has given way to a new openness and cooperation. Parishes too must participate in the ecumenical movement, "whose purpose is the restoration of unity among all Christians, which the Church is bound by the will of Christ to promote" (c. 755; see Jn 17:20–21).

Some parishes go so far as to enter into covenants with nearby Protestant congregations to maximize their cooperative interaction. They try to do everything possible together, from worship to social programs. In the process they not only break down prejudices and foster understanding, but they magnify their joint Christian witness "that the world might believe."

Other parishes engage in occasional ecumenical services, for example, on Thanksgiving, during the week of prayer for Christian unity, on Palm Sunday, or they hold joint choir performances or pulpit exchanges. Some Catholic and Protestant congregations cosponsor youth programs, adult education programs, counseling centers, food banks, clothing drives, shelters for the homeless and housing for the elderly.

Such cooperation and the conversations that surround it do not foster indifferentism or religious neutrality; rather they tend to sharpen a community's own identity as well as to heighten appreciation for the strengths of another tradition. They help to break down the scandal of a divided Christianity and enlarge the areas of common witness. There is no reason why active ecumeni-cal engagement cannot work alongside vigorous efforts to evan-gelize the unchurched in the area.

Parish and the City

Catholic parishes are very stable and enduring. They are often mainstays in their neighborhoods or towns. They, the communi-ties in addition to the church buildings, continue long after many other neighborhood landmarks or institutions have passed on. Parishes tend to be stabilizing elements within the larger commu-nity of the neighborhood or town, but they can also be agents of change and revitalization.

Parish communities, like the lay Catholics who populate them, have commitments to "the earthly city," and must have suitable freedom to pursue those commitments (c. 227). Parishes too "are bound by a special duty to imbue and perfect the order of tempo-ral affairs with the spirit of the gospel" (c. 225.2). They may not remain aloof from their surrounding human communities; they must strive to assist and improve them.

In the 1988 *Apostolic Exhortation on the Laity,* Pope John Paul II said:

> If indeed the parish is the church placed in the neighborhoods of
> humanity, it lives and is at work through being deeply inserted in
> human society and intimately bound up with its aspirations and its
> dramatic events. Oftentimes the social context, especially in cer-
> tain countries and environments, is violently shaken by elements
> of disintegration and dehumanization. The individual is lost and
> disoriented, but there always remains in the human heart the
> desire to experience and cultivate caring and personal relation-
> ships. The response to such a desire can come from the parish
> when, with the lay faithful's participation, it adheres to its funda-
> mental vocation and mission, that is, to be a "place" in the world
> for the community of believers to gather together as a "sign" and
> "instrument" of the vocation of all to communion, in a word, to be
> a house of welcome to all and a place of service to all or, as Pope
> John XXIII was fond of saying, to be the "village fountain" to
> which all would have recourse in their thirst. (*CL* 27)

Social action and community development are more and more a part of today's parish agenda. The parish community should be engaged with the social problems around it. It should be a part of efforts to promote social justice, to eliminate racial and ethnic discrimination, to combat crime and drug abuse, to encourage housing for the poor and elderly, to improve public education, to curb violence and develop alternative dispute resolution and to stabilize employment opportunities.

The parish should not be politically partisan; usually that is divisive and alienating in the long run. But the parish should promote voting and other forms of active political involvement by its members. The local church has a major stake in the local community. It must make its values and voice heard in the decisions and policies of that community.

Sources and Readings

Confer the canonical literature cited after Chapter 5. Also:

Pontifical Council for Promoting Christian Unity. *Directory for the Application of Principles and Norms on Ecumenism*, March 25, 1993. *Origins* 23, 9 (July 29, 1993):129–60.

10
Parishes in American Law

Catholic parishes are subject to federal and state laws under the American legal system. They must obey statutes enacted by legislatures and other rule-making bodies, for example, city councils or county commissioners, and they are within the jurisdiction of the courts and subject to the police powers of the government.

The Constitution of the United States of America guarantees the free exercise of religion and prohibits the establishment of any religion. Within these two parameters the delicate balance of church-state relations is worked out by legislatures and courts. The extent of permissible government assistance to church-sponsored enterprises is frequently in contention, for example, public aid to religious schools, released or shared time arrangements, tuition tax credits. And the scope of religious freedom has often been tested, for example, the legitimacy of religious schools and the standards within them, access to and use of public school facilities for religious purposes. By and large the American constitutional context of free exercise and non-establishment of religion has proven to be very congenial to the life and growth of local churches.

The purpose of this chapter is to provide a brief overview of the various categories and kinds of legal regulations that parishes and other local congregations may encounter or must observe. The chapter intends to heighten awareness of the multiple facets of American law so that parish communities can then seek out the legal counsel they need.

Ownership of Parish Property

State law governs the way the churches may organize themselves for the acquisition and ownership of property as well as for other legal activities. Most states allow some form of incorporation for religious organizations. However, the way that the actual title and control of parish property are held varies depending on the laws of the state and the choices made at the time the diocese and parish were established.

1. The parish property may be a part of a unified diocesan property-holding structure as

a. a "corporation sole" in which the diocesan bishop as an incorporated office holds title to all of the property of all of the parishes in the diocese;

b. a "nonprofit religious corporation" that holds all of the parish properties within the diocese, and the bishop is the only member of the corporation;

c. a "charitable trust" that holds all of the parish properties, of which the bishop is the sole trustee and holds the property in trust for the beneficiaries, the people of the parishes;

d. a "fee simple" in which the bishop personally holds all of the property in his own name.

All of these unified holding structures have the same difficulty: they are at odds with the canonical system, which puts the ownership and control of church property in the hands of the juridical person that acquired it (c. 1256), meaning that parish property is owned by the parish, not the diocese. They centralize the property of the parishes in the hands of the bishop and lead him to act as though he can dispose of it at will. Also such a unified pool of property is a tempting target for those who "go after the deep pockets" (see tort claims, below).

2. The parish may hold its own property

a. as a separate membership corporation in which, for example, the diocesan bishop, the vicar general, the pastor and two laypersons are the members of the corporation, and no action with regard to the disposal of property can be taken without the agreement of the bishop and vicar general;

b. as a separately incorporated nonprofit religious corporation;

c. as a charitable trust with the pastor as trust administrator of the property and the people of the parish as the beneficiaries of the trust;

d. as an unincorporated religious association that is recognized by the state as able to hold and control property.

Obviously, it is essential to know what forms of religious organization property-holding structures are permitted in the state and which one is actually being employed by the church. In adjudicating church property disputes the civil courts will honor the law of the state and the form of property holding actually in effect.

American civil courts usually consider the Roman Catholic Church to be hierarchical (rather than congregational) in its structure, and they tend to respect its clearly delineated ascending levels of church authority.

Ministerial Status

For the purposes of some federal and state laws the status of "ordained, commissioned, or licensed ministers of the church" is important. Both federal income tax laws and social security legislation grant some benefits to persons in these categories, for example, a nontaxed housing allowance, exemption from withholding, self-employed status. These same laws apply "to services performed in the exercise of ministry," that is, to the person's activities as a minister.

Other instances in which this issue of ministerial status is crucial are the area of confidential communications, that is, the "clergy-penitent privilege," which permits one to refuse to disclose revelations made in the context of confession or spiritual counseling. Another is the state-authorized performance of marriage ceremonies. In addition, some states exempt ministers from jury duty and grant them visiting privileges at penal institutions. These matters are governed by state statutes, and the states differ greatly in their provisions regarding them.

While the status of ordained priests and deacons is clear in the Catholic tradition, the status of many lay ministers functioning in Catholic parishes is not as well determined. Those who are officially assigned and perform traditional ministries, for example, preaching, leading liturgical prayer, distributing holy communion, baptizing and conducting funerals, may be recognized by the courts as belonging to this legally recognized category.

Parish Liability: Contracts, Torts, Agency

Liability is legally enforceable responsibility. A parish may be obligated to pay for its contracted goods and services, for its breaches of contractual duties or for the tortious activity, for example, negligent personal injury or property damage, of someone acting on its behalf. In both instances, contract and tort, the key is agency, that is, is the person who made the contract or committed the tort authorized to act on behalf of the parish?

A contract is a mutual agreement for goods or services, involving an offer and an acceptance. A tort is a legal wrong committed on a person or on property. A tort can be unintentional, through negligence, like an auto accident or a fall on icy steps, or intentional, that is, deliberately inflicted, like sexual misconduct or defamation of character.

In matters of contract the key issue is who has the authority to enter into contracts on behalf of the parish, for example, who can hire or fire people, who can order and pay for supplies and maintenance. Was the pastor or associate or business manager or janitor acting within the parameters of his or her authority? The pastor's authority is clear (c. 532); that of others may be less so.

Contract law is one area in which the church "canonizes" local civil law. That is to say, canon law explicitly requires that the local civil law of contracts be observed and honored (c. 1290).

In matters of tort the issue is whether the parish is answerable for the actions of the person who committed the wrong. Employers are often held liable for the actions of their employees ("respondeat superior"), but usually only when the employees are acting within the scope of their employment. Was the action reasonably connected with the work of the employee, or was the employee "on a frolic of his own"? An act of adultery or of sexual abuse can hardly be viewed as an action within the scope of employment of a sacred minister.

At this writing (1996) "clergy malpractice" is not a tort recognized by American courts. There are constitutional difficulties in trying to determine the "standards of the profession" for clergy, against which tortious actions would be measured. However, some clerical misconduct has been charged under different rubrics, for example, invasion of privacy, outrageous conduct or breach of fiduciary duty.

In addition to the responsibility of the parish, the question of "ascending liability" arises, that is, the possible liability of the diocese for actions of parish personnel. Is the parish a real community with appropriate autonomy and subsidiary function, or, by "piercing the corporate veil," is it revealed to be a mere arm or totally controlled part of the diocese? A court might decide either way.

The Parish as Employer

As an organization that employs persons, the parish is subject to many federal and state regulations, many of which were enacted for the benefit and protection of employees. Each statute or legislative act must be examined separately to see whether it applies to parishes or whether it grants an exemption for religious organizations. Some statutes are related to interstate commerce or apply only to employers of a certain number of employees.

Virtually all employers are obliged to withhold income taxes and social security taxes.

Churches are subject to laws against discrimination in employment. The federal Civil Rights Act of 1964 forbids discrimination in employment because of race, color, religion, sex or national origin, but it contains an exemption for religious discrimination by religious employers. The exemption can extend not only to the professed religious faith of the employees but also to their adherence or practice of that faith. The religious exemption has been construed to apply even to secretarial and custodial employees. The Civil Rights Act provides another exemption for positions in which religion is a "bona fide occupational qualification" necessary for normal operation.

Churches are not exempt from the provisions of the Civil Rights Act that forbid discrimination based on sex, and this includes the prohibition of sexual harassment. The Equal Pay Act of 1963 forbids employers from paying a lower wage rate to employees of one sex than another for equal work at jobs requiring the same skill, effort and responsibility and performed under similar working conditions.

The free exercise clause of the Constitution protects churches in their selection and treatment, for example, tenure in office or reimbursement, of clergy. This protection may not always extend to all other ministers.

Churches are not exempt from the provisions of the laws that prohibit discrimination based on race, color, national origin, age (Age Discrimination Employment Act, 1975) or disability (Americans with Disabilities Act, 1990). Acceptance of federal funding for projects or programs can subject religious organizations to increased levels of federal control.

The National Labor Relations Act (1935), which assures employees the right to join a union and engage in collective bargaining, does not contain any exemptions for religious organizations, but the Supreme Court has held (1979) that teachers in church-run schools are not covered by the act because of the risk that the church's First Amendment rights might be infringed by the government's inquiry into the schools' labor practices and because of the sensitive issues of the relationships between the schools and their sponsoring religious body. Some state labor relations legislation has been ruled to apply to teachers in church-sponsored schools. Religious organizations that engage in commercial activities, for example, hospitals, nursing homes and colleges, in which the propagation of doctrine, belief and religious practice is not a pervasive part of the mission probably are subject to the NLRA in those enterprises.

The Fair Labor Standards Act (1938) protects workers from substandard wages and excessive hours and regulates child labor. It requires time-and-a-half pay for hours over forty per week and sets a minimum wage. The act includes schools and hospitals in its coverage. Religious organizations are not specifically exempted from the act, but churches performing entirely religious functions and not engaged in commercial activities are not usually subject to it.

The Immigration Reform and Control Act (1986) requires employers to verify the employment eligibility of job applicants. This is done by means of documents such as driver's licenses, social security cards, birth certificates or resident alien cards. The act also bans discrimination against noncitizens by employers of four or more workers. There is no religious exemption from the act.

The Occupational Safety and Health Act (1970) requires employers to maintain safe and health-protected workplaces. Employers subject to the act are those engaged in a business affecting commerce, that is, trade, traffic, commerce, transportation or communication among the states. There are no exemptions for churches or religious organizations.

Some state and local laws ban discrimination based on sexual orientation or related to jury duty or military reserve training. Some may exempt religious organizations, others do not. Likewise local legislation may require employers to establish policies regarding smoking in the workplace. Local legal counsel should be consulted on all of these matters.

The Parish as Property Owner

Property ownership is regulated by state property laws, and they apply to religious organizations the same as to others. The control of the use of land is one of the police powers of the state.

Zoning ordinances are the means used by municipalities to control the various uses, for example, residential or commercial, to which land may be put, as well as the kinds of structures that may be erected on it. The ordinances often provide for such things as historic districts, flood plains, wetlands or other conservation areas. Churches and their related schools and activities must comply with local zoning ordinances or request exceptions or variances from the appropriate commission or board.

Municipal planning boards or commissions sometimes impose further land-use regulations in the interests of the orderly development of communities in accord with long-range master plans. They review such things as subdivisions of land, laying out new streets or closing existing ones, and constructing drainage systems. They review site plans for such things as adequacy of access roads, parking, sidewalks and placement of buildings. Parish plans are subject to review by such planning boards like other land-use developments.

Building codes impose construction standards for purposes of health, safety and sanitation. Churches are subject to building codes and can be compelled to comply with them.

The Americans with Disabilities Act imposes certain standards of handicapped access to public accommodations, but it exempts religious organizations, including places of worship. Parishes will probably wish to comply even though not required to do so.

Landmark designations for cultural or historical reasons are sometimes imposed by municipal agencies, and they have the effect of limiting the structural alterations that may be made without prior approval. Hence they can cause a burden on a parish in its efforts to manage or maintain its buildings and property as it desires. Conflicts involving landmark designations are resolved by courts weighing free exercise of religion rights against the legitimate police powers of the state.

Environmental concerns sometimes impinge on local churches when they acquire land that has hazardous wastes or petroleum contamination, for example, a leaking underground fuel tank, or when one of their buildings contains insulation or construction materials made with asbestos. Religious institutions are not exempt from compliance to environmental laws and must act with great care in complying with them. It goes without saying that clean air and water and the elimination of toxic substances are moral as well as legal concerns, but liabilities can be strict and clean-up costs very high.

Eminent domain is the power of the government—federal, state and local—to take private property for public use, for example, to take land in order to build a highway. The owner of the property must be justly compensated, which usually means the owner should receive fair market value for the property. Churches can have their property taken for these governmental purposes, although religious freedom may limit the state's exercise of eminent domain in certain circumstances.

Leases of buildings or property owned by a local church can have serious legal implications, and the terms of the leases should be scrutinized by knowledgeable counsel. Leasing church property for nonchurch uses, for example, a day-care center, may subject it to state or federal taxes on "unrelated business income." Leases also may carry with them property taxes and other burdens of maintenance, repair and insurance. The leased property may be subject to nondiscrimination or handicapped access regulations that do not apply to the parish itself.

The exemption of churches and church-related properties from property taxes is a nationwide and historically honored practice, and it has been declared to be constitutional, that is, it does not imply government establishment of religion (Supreme Court, 1970). The exemption reflects an age-old benevolent neutrality on the part of the government toward churches and religious practice. State laws vary on the scope of the exemption, for example, whether it includes parsonages, rectories and convents, as well as houses of religious worship, under what conditions and up to what dollar amount. Property owned by a church but used for other purposes may be subject to property taxation. The extent of churches' exemption from property taxes has been the subject of much litigation.

Churches sometimes make voluntary contributions to municipalities in lieu of taxes in order to make some compensation for the services and benefits that the church receives from the municipality, for example, police and fire protection, use of streets and sewers. It may be a matter of equity, or simply good public relations, but it should also be done with care so as not to create an expectation that may not always be met.

Copyright Law

Copyrights, which are grounded in the Constitution, exist to promote the progress of science and the arts. They protect the rights of creators of music, literature, art and other works to be compensated for the fruit of their labors. Religious music, writings, translations, dramas, artworks and computer software share in the protection of the federal Copyright Act (1976).

Copyrights obtained after 1977 endure for the life of the author plus fifty years. Violations of the law in the form of copyright infringements carry severe penalties. Churches have a moral obligation to observe the laws of copyright, but their nonobservance may also subject them to significant penalties. The most common copyright infringement is making multiple copies of a work without permission or payment of fees. Churches can easily obtain authorization from the copyright owner. Music publishers have generous policies regarding church music; some grant blanket licenses to churches for a modest annual fee.

Many historic and classical compositions of church music have long since passed into the public domain and are no longer covered by copyright, even though they may have been recently republished.

The Parish and Federal Income Taxes

Nonprofit religious, charitable and educational organizations have long enjoyed exemption from federal income taxes. It is not a constitutional right, however, and religious organizations must secure and maintain their tax exempt status. Section 501(c)(3) of the Internal Revenue Code creates the exemption for religious and other groups. Churches are not required to file an application for the exemption as many other nonprofit groups are, nor are churches required to file annual information returns. However, this federal tax exemption carries with it restrictions on the following two political activities:

1. Lobbying. No substantial part of the organization's activity may be carrying on propaganda or otherwise attempting to influence legislation. (Furthermore, contributions to organizations with substantial lobbying activities are not tax deductible.)

2. Political Campaigns. The exempt organization is not to participate or intervene in any political campaign on behalf of or in opposition to any candidate for public office (national, state or local). Parishes may engage in political activities, but they must be neutral with regard to candidates, that is, they must not make statements for or endorse one over another, or give financial contributions, solicit funds or make mailing lists or facilities available

for one candidate and not others. Parishes may make facilities available to all candidates, engage in voter education, sponsor public forums or debates to which all parties are invited, encourage parishioner involvement, even criticize public officials, but such activities must be neutral as to individual candidates.

Unrelated business income earned by religious organizations that are exempt from federal income tax is taxable. When the unrelated business activity is substantial, is carried on regularly and is not related to the exempt purposes of the church or organization, then the income from it is taxable. This is a highly technical area of federal tax law, and qualified experts should be consulted.

The Internal Revenue Service may only begin a tax inquiry of a church if a high-level Treasury official (i.e., the Secretary or delegate) reasonably believes, on the basis of written records, that the church may not be exempt, may be engaged in unrelated business or may be otherwise engaged in taxable activity. This strong restraint on IRS tax audits of churches resulted from Section 7611 added by Congress to the Internal Revenue Code. It affects inquiries begun after 1984, but it does not include criminal investigations or certain routine inquiries.

Contributions to churches are deductible for federal income tax purposes (Section 170 of the Internal Revenue Code). The contributions must be of cash or property (not services rendered), deductible in the year in which they were given, unconditional gifts, without any personal benefit to the donor. The contributions are deductible only if they are verified or substantiated, and their amount is subject to certain limitations, for example, up to 50 percent of the taxpayer's adjusted gross income.

The Parish and Other Laws

State income taxes, where they exist, most often exempt religious organizations, as the federal income tax system does. Unrelated business income earned by religious groups is usually subject to taxation, as it is with the IRS.

Churches are frequently exempt from state sales taxes (and the concomitant use taxes on goods purchased in another state) imposed on personal property sales and services. The parameters and requirements of the exemptions vary from state to state.

States have recently enacted some form of "reporting statutes," that is, laws that require certain categories of persons to report to public authorities knowledge of actual or suspected child abuse. The authorities are responsible for any further investigation or action. The persons reporting are generally protected from civil or criminal liability as long as they made the report in good faith, but failing to report can subject them to criminal penalties. The state statutes vary greatly on many points, especially on the categories of persons required to do the reporting; for example, some explicitly exclude priests and ministers, while others implicitly include them. (Revelations made in sacramental confession, covered by the seal of the confessional, may pose a conflict with those statutes including priests. See cc. 983–984, 1388.) Nonordained ministers, for example, pastoral counselors, youth ministers, teachers, day-care providers, are more likely to be included among those required to report child abuse.

State and local laws regarding the sale and serving of food to the public apply to churches and affiliated organizations, for example, parish-sponsored soup kitchens, bake sales, bazaars. Such food and health laws can be very detailed. Knowledge of the nature and extent of local regulations is strongly advised.

This overview of American laws that apply to or may affect local Catholic congregations is only a beginning. It makes no claim to completeness; for instance, most criminal law has been omitted. The chapter only serves as a preliminary notice to parishes about possible areas of legal complications. Local legal counsel should be sought when actual problems or opportunities emerge.

One final word of caution: canon law requires that before filing a legal suit or responding to one on behalf of a parish the diocesan bishop be notified (c. 1288). Common sense would normally call for the same action, especially in these days when diocesan insurance plans or diocesan attorneys may provide legal representation.

Sources and Readings

Bartlett, C. *The Tenure of Parochial Property in the United States of America.* Canon Law Studies, no. 31. Washington, D.C.: Catholic University of America, 1926.

Couser, R. *Ministry and the American Legal System.* Minneapolis: Fortress Press, 1993.

Dignan, P. *A History of the Legal Incorporation of Catholic Church Property in the United States (1784–1932).* Studies in American Church History, no. 14. Washington, D.C.: Catholic University of America, 1933.

Donovan, T. *The Status of the Church in American Civil and Canon Law.* Canon Law Studies, no. 446. Washington, D.C.: Catholic University of America, 1966.

Eidsmoe, J. *The Christian Legal Advisor.* Milford, Mich.: Mott Media, 1984.

Hammar, R. *Pastor, Church and Law.* 2nd ed. Matthews, N.C.: Christian Ministry Resources, 1991.

Ioppolo, D., et al. *Confidentiality in the United States: A Legal and Canonical Study.* Washington, D.C.: CLSA, 1988.

Maida, A., and N. Cafardi. *Church Property, Church Finances, and Church-Related Corporations: A Canon Law Handbook.* St. Louis: Catholic Health Association, 1984.

Mazur, C., and R. Bullis. *Legal Guide for Day-to-Day Church Matters: A Handbook for Pastors and Church Members.* Cleveland: United Church, 1994.

McMenamin, R., and W. Kralovec. *Clergy & Teacher Malpractice: Recognition and Prevention.* Portland, Ore.: Jomac Publishing, 1987.

Conclusion

Lex Orandi, Lex Credendi

"The law of worship is the law of belief" is a reliable maxim that has been a solid part of Christian tradition since the fifth century. It means that the words, gestures and patterns of the church's worship are a good indication of the church's beliefs. The rule of prayer is the rule of faith.

One very obvious feature of the church's prayer is that it is almost exclusively voiced in the plural. "*Our* Father," "let *us* pray," "*we* call to mind," "have mercy on *us*," "grant *us* peace," "*we* believe." Virtually all of the church's public worship is spoken or sung in the plural because it is meant to be prayed *together*, in the assembly of the faithful, in community. The church's plural prayer form is a forceful indication that the church is communal, is made up of communities. Christians, especially Catholic Christians, are not isolated individuals but live and pray in communities of disciples.

The church exists first and foremost in local congregations gathered for worship and witness. These local communities, parishes and other communities, are the living embodiments of the church. This book has tried to recall that basic fact and present the roots and reasons for it.

121

Vatican II

The most solemn teaching document of the Second Vatican Council, the *Dogmatic Constitution on the Church,* stated:

> This church of Christ is truly present in all legitimate local congregations of the faithful, which...are themselves called churches in the New Testament. For in their locality these are the new people called by God, in the Holy Spirit....In them the faithful are gathered together by the preaching of the gospel of Christ, and the mystery of the Lord's Supper is celebrated....In these communities...Christ is present. By His power the one, holy, catholic and apostolic church is gathered together. (*LG* 26)

The passage refers unmistakably to parishes and other local churches *within* the diocese.

This statement is at the heart of the church's official theology of the local church. This book was written to raise up that theology, to show where it came from and what it implies, especially for the canonical rules on the parish.

A Challenge to Parishes

Pope John Paul II, in an address to a group of American bishops on July 2, 1993, gave this challenge to parishes:

> One of the strengths of the church in the United States has always been the role of the parish as the focal point not only of the sacramental life but also of Catholic formation and education, of charitable and social activity....A great effort is needed by priests and laity to renew parish life in the image of the church herself as a communion benefiting from the complementary gifts and charisms of all her members. Communion is a dynamic reality which implies a constant exchange of gifts and services between all the members of the people of God. The vitality of a parish depends on merging the diverse vocations and gifts of its members into a unity which manifests the communion of each one and of all together with God the Father through Christ, constantly renewed by the grace of the Holy Spirit.

This vision of vital and dynamic parish communities calls for freedom of expression, mutual respect and generous collaboration. It is communities such as these that made up the communion of Christ's church in the first century and make it up today. The challenge to today's parishes is to respond to this vision and never cease striving to recreate it.

The author hopes that this study will help in some small way to assist in the renewal of parish life through a deeper understanding of the nature and dignity, the rights and responsibilities, the strength and genius, of the local church.

Case Studies

The case-study method can be a valuable and effective way of learning. Groups, such as parish staffs or parish councils, can come together over issues like these, grapple with the problems they pose and get to know one another in the reflection process. The following cases, followed by questions, are provided for such purposes of study and reflection.

St. Joseph's Parish and Father Steele

Father Sweet had been the pastor of St. Joseph's for ten years when Bishop Brophy asked him to move to another parish. He hadn't been an ideal pastor: parish income hadn't kept pace with inflation, the church building was beginning to suffer from deferred maintenance and the parish school had closed during his time as pastor. But Father Sweet was a "people person." He related well, trusted the laity, supported their initiatives and promoted good liturgical celebrations. He worked closely with the parish council, and that group became the effective leadership focus of the parish.

Bishop Brophy assigned Father Steele to replace Father Sweet at St. Joseph's, even though Steele was known to be a "law and order" priest, and people had complained about his authoritarian style at his last parish. The bishop didn't have many choices, and he thought that the finances and physical plant needed attention at St. Joseph's. He urged Steele to work collaboratively with the people as Sweet had.

Steele was young and vigorous. He worked out in the gym every day. He regarded himself as a natural leader and was not given to self-doubt. He played by the rules, said his prayers and worked at preaching well.

As soon as he arrived, Steele fired the janitor and the house-keeper and hired new ones, and he had all the locks changed on all the buildings. He made an assessment of needed repairs and began to talk to the people about the money to pay for them. He met with the parish council and laid out his agenda. The council responded very unenthusiastically and came back with a plan of their own. Steele soon stopped consulting the council, then he postponed their regular meetings as well as the election of new members.

Father Steele sought to economize by not replacing the liturgical coordinator when she resigned and by cutting the music budget in half. Eucharistic celebrations became more perfunctory and less participative.

The members of the parish council, after trying to reason with Father Steele and being rebuffed, appealed to Bishop Brophy about Steele's attitude toward them. They received a letter back from the chancellor of the diocese telling them that in canon law the pastor is responsible for the parish, and that the parish council has only an advisory function.

What actions could the parish council take?

What steps would you suggest to them?

St. Mary's Parish and Sister Jane

The availability of priests in the Diocese of Plains had steadily declined, and Bishop Novak was compelled to seek out someone else to head St. Mary's Parish in Tinyville after old Father Gilhooly died. Sister Jane Reynolds, OSB, who had several years of pastoral experience in other parishes, applied for the position, and the bishop gave her a five-year contract to lead the parish. She was the first nonpriest to be appointed to head a parish in the diocese, so everyone was a little uncertain about procedures and authority.

The first couple of years were very difficult for Sister Jane and for the parish. Father Smith would come over from Centerville, fifty miles away, to celebrate the eucharist twice a month. The people were not comfortable with the word and communion service that Jane led on the other Sundays.

Jane was a strong person and a good minister, however, and gradually the people got used to her and appreciated her talents and her dedication to them. A few families continued to avoid St. Mary's and drive over to Centerville for mass on Sundays, but a majority of the parishioners accepted Jane as the leader of the parish community and became devoted to her as their pastor.

Jane preached at the Sunday services, even when Father Smith was there for mass, as well as at funerals and weddings, and she usually baptized the children and adult converts in the parish. One time, when she couldn't find a priest anywhere in the county, she anointed a woman who was dying. She carefully explained to the woman that she was not a priest, but the woman was greatly consoled by her ministry and died peacefully a few hours later. Her family was reconciled to the church as a result.

Jane's ministerial actions were reported to Bishop Novak as liturgical abuses, and he felt constrained to remove Sister Jane from her position at St. Mary's .

What are the avenues open to Sister Jane?

What could the parish community do?

Holy Cross Parish and Father Miller

Father Miller was an independent and enterprising priest of the old school. He was a man of action. When it became obvious to him that Holy Cross Parish, in a thriving resort community, needed a larger church, he went ahead and built one. He borrowed the money from a local banker. He didn't tell the bishop or anyone else in the diocese about it; the first the bishop knew about the new church was when Miller invited him to come and bless it.

In spite of his displeasure at not having been asked for permission to build a new parish church, the bishop was forced to admire the spacious and handsome multipurpose building that Father Miller showed him. It seemed to suit the parish's needs.

The bishop asked Father Miller how he got so much for his money and how his relatively small congregation was going to pay off the debt.

Father Miller proudly informed the bishop that he had worked out some special arrangements with the contractor: no union labor was used on the project; they avoided accident insurance and workman's compensation; they did not do environmental impact studies, did not comply with state requirements for minority subcontractors and used some building materials that did not conform to code. These measures added up to real savings in construction costs.

Miller explained that he was earning extra income for the parish in order to pay down the construction debt by renting the church to the local Methodist congregation for a service on Sunday mornings, and to the Jewish temple community on Friday evenings. He also rented the building to musical groups, jazz and rock, on other evenings, and the parish bingo game was held each week, even though it was not allowed in that jurisdiction.

What is your judgment about Father Miller's dealings, both in the construction project and in fund-raising activities?

What can the parish community do about them?

The Merger of All Saints and Saint Anne's

Just one year after Bishop Harrison praised All Saints, on the occasion of its one hundredth anniversary, as a strong and vibrant parish, he announced that it would be merged with Saint Anne's downtown, and its church closed. Both parishes originated as French national churches, and many of their parishioners still preferred to worship in French.

The bishop gave two reasons for his decision: a declining number of priests able to serve French-speaking communities and the need for expensive repairs to All Saints church. The church, which had been built more than sixty years before, was like a cathedral, very large and ornate. However, much of the exterior brickwork had deteriorated, and repairs were estimated to cost around

$500,000. The bishop felt that the declining and aging parish community should not be burdened with expenses of that magnitude.

The parishioners were extraordinarily devoted to their parish and its handsome church. They organized to try to change the bishop's judgment by every means available. They carried on their struggle year after year. They formed committees, met repeatedly with diocesan officials and presented their case before a special reconciliation panel. They appealed through the church's administrative system to the Congregation of Clergy in Rome, from there to the Apostolic Signatura (the church's high court) and from an ordinary panel of judges in that court to a plenary session. They appealed, on the basis of property ownership and due process, through the local and state civil courts, all the way up to the United States Supreme Court. All to no avail.

Throughout the long processes of negotiations and legal recourse, the community retained its own cohesion, loyalty and hope. They met every Sunday for prayer across the street from their closed church or in the nearby United Church. They persevered, and maintained an exceptional spirit of civility and Christian charity in their communications. They were intent on remaining in communion with the bishop and the diocese.

Bishop Harrison retired, and Bishop O'Riley was appointed in his place. He reached out to the All Saints community, celebrated mass with them and proposed a new response to their petitions. He said that the parishes would remain merged but that services could be held at both sites, that is, at Saint Anne's church and at a hall on the property of All Saints. He said that the parishioners of the merged parish could determine whether or not they could raise the money and go forward with the restoration of their cherished All Saints. The parishioners were overjoyed and felt that they had been delivered from exile.

What can be learned from this story?

What values were at stake on both sides?

The Five Parishes in Irontown

In 1995 there were five Catholic parishes in Irontown, a small city in Pennsylvania where about four thousand Catholics lived.

All of the parishes were ethnic in origin (Irish, Croatian, Italian, German and Slovenian), although one had been designated as the territorial parish. The oldest was founded in 1878, the most recent in 1909.

A new bishop was named in the diocese, and he announced that "we need to make the best use of our human and material resources." He launched a "Parish Clusters Consultation" process to look into possible mergers "in the context of shifting population within the diocese."

The outcome of the consultation process was the proposal to merge all five parishes in Irontown into one, Prince of Peace. The bishop implemented this decision by his decree of February 15, 1995: Assumption, St. Peter, St. Ann, St. James and St. John parishes were all extinguished, and their assets and liabilities went to the new territorial parish. Worship was to be conducted only at the former Assumption church, and St. Ann's school was chosen to serve the new parish community.

Two groups protested the decision most vigorously, the Croatians of Assumption Parish and the Vietnamese of St. James. They both had numerous recent immigrants within their communities and, consequently, had special ministerial needs. They asked that two churches remain open, rather than only one, and that priests of their language and tradition be retained in order to meet their spiritual needs.

The appeals of these two communities were met with courteous rejections: their issues had already been considered, their appeal was not made in time, some of those making the appeal lived outside parish boundaries.

Should viable parishes be closed for lack of priests?

When a parish is no longer viable, how can its ethnic groups be cared for?

Index

130

About the Author

James A. Coriden was born in Hammond, Indiana, in 1932. He was ordained a presbyter of the Diocese of Gary in 1957. He earned a bachelor's degree at St. Meinrad Seminary and a licentiate in theology and a doctorate in canon law at the Gregorian University in Rome. He later received the Juris Doctor from the Columbus School of Law at The Catholic University of America.

Father Coriden served in parishes, in the tribunal and in the chancery of the Diocese of Gary from 1961 to 1968. He taught on the faculty of theology at The Catholic University from 1968 to 1975. Since that time he has served on the faculty of the Washington Theological Union as Professor of Canon Law.

The author has been an active member of the Canon Law Society of America since 1961. He organized and published several interdisciplinary symposia for the society, served on its board of governors and was one of the general editors and authors of *The Code of Canon Law: A Text and Commentary*, commissioned by the society after the promulgation of the 1983 Code. The society granted him its Role of Law Award in 1987. He is also a longtime member of the Canadian Canon Law Society and the International Association for the Promotion of the Study of Canon Law.

Father Coriden has published *An Introduction to Canon Law* (Mahwah, N.J.: Paulist Press, London: Geoffrey Chapman, 1991) and many articles on canonical topics, especially in the areas of the rights of church members, ministry, parishes, the teaching authority and the interpretation of canons.